What they're saying about Dan Dunn and his book . . .

"Welcome to the weird and wacky world of Dan Dunn. He now lays claim to being one of the funniest and most cunning rascals in the dirty trenches of journalism. This is the first of many wonderful books to come."

—Douglas Brinkley, author of *The Great Deluge*

"Dan Dunn is a fanatical party monster who is a danger to himself and anyone who crosses his path. The funny thing is—and I do mean funny—he's lived to write about it. If I don't get to direct the movie version of *Nobody Likes a Quitter*, I'm firing my agent."

—Danny Leiner, director of *Dude, Where's My Car?*
and *Harold and Kumar Go to White Castle*

"Dan Dunn's writing has always been droll and dripping with inebriated humor from his well-lubricated editorials in the Aspen, Colorado, daily papers to his sloshed blogs on the Internet. I first met him passed out on the floor, at the feet of my former neighbor, the late Hunter S. Thompson, and have been waiting for him to sober up enough to finish this damn book ever since!"

—John Oates of the rock duo Hall & Oates

"Every time I read the literary genius that IS Dan Dunn, I'm floored. But then, I pick myself up off the floor, crawl back up on my barstool, and crack open another box of wine. He makes me feel so smart."

—Mark Steines, host of *Entertainment Tonight*

"As a health and nutrition writer, I have failed at many attempts to explain how Dan Dunn is still alive. Imbiber is too kind of a description for Dan. The man has drunk from a fire hose and has distilled ambrosia from this so that we ourselves might civilly imbibe. To steal a phrase from Fleetwood Mac, Dan Dunn makes lovin' fun."

—Christopher Wanjek, author of *Food at Work* and *Bad Medicine*

"Dan Dunn is a maniac. If you see him coming your way, for the love of God, buy him a drink and listen to some of his stories. Just don't let him sleep at your house. He'll pee on your couch. If you don't think this book is funny then your opinion on anything no longer matters."

—Rob McElhenney, creator and star of *It's Always Sunny in Philadelphia*

"Dan is both knowledgeable and self deprecating. His stories about the things that alcohol makes one do are so wickedly raw and funny it may have you reconsider drinking alcohol altogether."

—Dominique Paul, author of *The Possibility of Fireflies*

Nobody Likes a Quitter
(and other reasons to avoid rehab)

The Loaded Life of an Outlaw Booze Writer

⋅ ♈ ♈ ♈ ⋅

DAN DUNN

Thunder's Mouth Press
New York

NOBODY LIKES A QUITTER (AND OTHER REASONS TO AVOID REHAB):
The Loaded Life of an Outlaw Booze Writer

Thunder's Mouth Press
An imprint of Avalon Publishing Group Inc.

AVALON
publishing group incorporated

Copyright © 2007 by Dan Dunn

Thunder's Mouth Press books are available at special discounts for bulk purchases in the United States by corporations, institutions, and other organizations. For more information, please contact the Special Markets Department at the Perseus Books Group, 2300 Chestnut Street, Suite 200, Philadelphia, PA 19103, or call (800) 255-1514, or e-mail special.markets@perseusbooks.com

Library of Congress Cataloging-in-Publication Data

Dunn, Dan, 1968-
Nobody likes a quitter (and other reasons to avoid rehab) : the loaded life of an outlaw booze writer / Dan Dunn.
p. cm.
Includes bibliographical references and index.
ISBN 978-1-56858-366-2 (alk. paper)
1. Alcoholism--United States. 2. Drinking of alcoholic beverages--Social aspects--United States. I. Title.
HV5292.D86 2007
362.292092--DC22
2007012967

9 8 7 6 5 4 3 2 1

Interior design by Bettina Wilhelm

Printed in the United States of America
Distributed by Publishers Group West

This book is dedicated to Donna, Curtis,
and Finnegan Robinson

. . . and to the Clash, for "Junco Partner"

Contents

Author's Note
xi

-Step 1-
Into the Spirit of Things: How a Quasi-Degenerate
Booze Writer Is Born
1

-Step 2-
When They Say, "You'll Need Shots" to Go to Some Countries,
They Don't Mean the Kind at the Airport Bar
23

-Step 3-
Whisky: Proudly Destroying Livers Since 1088
47

-Step 4-
The Tequila Sunrise Also Rises
(Provided You Drink Too Many)
75

-Step 5-
Getting Boozy . . . and the Beast
99

-Step 6-
You Know What They Say About Guys with Small Chapters . . .
113

-Step 7-
A Woman of Some Importance
121

-Step 8-
Chick Drinks and the Men Who Drink Them
143

-Step 9-
Brushes with Celebrities, Comb-Overs with Nobodies
167

-Step 10-
What Would Jesus Drink? A Holiday Hootch Guide
191

-Step 11-
I'm Only Hanging On to Watch You Go Down
207

-Step 12-
Congratulations, You've Completed the Program and
Are Now Eligible to Begin a Far Less Glamorous One
223

Epilogue
235

Acknowledgments
237

About the Author
241

"Alcohol is the anesthesia by which we endure
the operation of life."
—George Bernard Shaw

Author's Note

In political circles, they say if you are the one explaining then you are the one losing. So I guess this is a concession speech of sorts—because Thunder's Mouth Press and I want you to know something going in: a few of the events recounted in these pages are what overzealous litterateurs and the Smoking Gun Web site might call "not historically accurate" or "subject to debate" or "remembered clearly, but may have been a dream." Hell, looking back, portions of this tome leave me sounding like one of the less lawyered-up members of the Bush administration. I guess some of the material has been either significantly embellished or wholly invented, and many of the characters herein are what the *Washington Post* would no doubt call "composites." What you're holding in your hands, dear reader, is a mosh pit of fact and fiction, with yours truly doing a bit of body surfing. But let me also add that, to the best of my knowledge, everything I've written pertaining to the history, production, promotion, and enjoyment of alcohol is on the level. Drinking is the part of my life where Truth reigns supreme. Unfortunately, there are parts of my life where drinking reigns supreme and parts of my Truth where life and drinking become one, a huge seven-headed beast and . . . wait, I'm sounding like the Bush administration again. Let me be blunt: I am, after all, in the employ of a large and reputable media conglomerate as one of the world's preeminent wine and spirits writers. As I lead you down the path to enlightenment about adult beverages, however, I am desperate that you somehow grasp just how brain-rattlingly inebriated I've kept myself throughout most of the past decade. I drink for a living, folks, and as a result my memory is foggier than a San Francisco morning after a Grateful Dead show; one of the early shows before the cops caught on. Plus, having grown up in a highly dysfunctional environment, as a coping mechanism I developed a vivid imagination that I now have a hell of a time keeping in check. For instance, I'm not entirely sure that I have, as reported in Step 9, partied with Chaka Khan. Then again, I'm not sure I *haven't*. The truth depends largely on the tenacity of her legal representation. Same goes for David Faustino and Polly Holliday. In fact, the same goes for anyone in this book, including those in the acknowledgments. *Especially* those people, because I always fear I'll end up drunk and homeless babbling to imaginary friends—oh, the people will actually exist, I'll just imagine they're my friends.

So perhaps it's best that you look upon the time spent reading this book as you would a visit to Mr. Rogers's Neighborhood— sometimes we'll be kicking it *real* in my house, only instead of sneakers and cardigan sweaters my closet will be full of liquor and skeletons. And whenever we need to spice things up a bit, we can always head to the Land of Make Believe . . . there's even a trolley to take us to and fro so we don't have to worry about getting another DUI.

So, let's make the most of this beautiful day. Since we're together, we might as well say: Would you be mine? Could you be mine? Won't you be my reader?

Cheers!

Dan Dunn
Los Angeles
April 9, 2007

Step 1

Into the Spirit of Things: How a Quasi-Degenerate Booze Writer Is Born

Four in the morning. A VIP table inside an exceedingly stylish night-club at the Wynn Hotel in Las Vegas. A ravishing young woman is on my lap, chatting up several other gorgeous ladies and occasionally leaning in to nibble on my ear. LapGal is a publicist for an exceedingly stylish high-demographic vodka that is usually marked up to around six or seven hundred dollars a bottle at places like this. We have three bottles on the table; two of them appear empty, though it's hard to know through the smoked glass. Our ample-bosomed, emerald-eyed hostess sashays over to the table and offers to top off my cocktail. I've had more than enough to drink over the past fourteen-odd hours, but I hold out my glass anyway. Common sense dictates that I should stop this, go back to my room, and sleep, but my incorrigible id propels me to keep going. A hedonistic mantra echoes in my head . . . *Nobody likes a quitter. Nobody likes a quitter. Nobody likes a quitter.*

"Are you having fun?" the hostess asks.

"Yes," I lie. "Lots of fun." Truth is, I feel kind of bored and a little nauseated and my vision has gone from merely blurry to that slight pre-room-spin phase. Just a few of many occupational hazards I'm routinely forced to contend with. Another one is the dreaded deadline, which in this case happens to be about, oh, five hours from now. You see, I'm what's known in the journalism biz as a "wine and spirits writer," and my employer is the world's largest newspaper company. While my friends always roll their eyes at the very idea of this drinking-and-scribbling as "work," I'm on the clock. My penchant for quoting Hunter S. Thompson—he noted that writing is like sex, mostly fun for amateurs—doesn't often help.

Then the hostess coos, "If you need anything—anything at all—just let me know," and suddenly, I feel a whole lot better.

"Oh, I will, darlin'," I reply, sliding her my phone number with a wink; she flashes a kittenish grin, and I immediately find myself lamenting having given LapGal a key to my complimentary suite. Then again, she's very sweet and has a large expense account at her disposal and, hell, maybe *she* digs the hostess, too. Perhaps nobody need be left out in the proverbial cold tonight. As LapGal settles what is surely an exceedingly stylish tab with her company credit card, I can't help but fantasize about how much fun the three of us could have together. We could all climb into the stretch limousine the hotel has generously provided and head over to a strip club to have lap dances and champagne and smoke expensive cigarettes. I'm not sure how LapGal would covertly slip that portion of the evening onto her credit card but maybe I could pick up some of the expense. I run that through my head, seeing the smoke billowing out of some newspaper accountant's ears, knowing it's a culture that has conference calls on cutting the paper-clip tab. But like that Booger guy in *Risky Business* put it, "Every now and then say, What the fuck" . . . so, What the fuck! "Stripper" sounds a lot like "paper" anyway—I'll list it under "office supplies." On second thought, perhaps it's best to skip the gentlemen's club altogether and take the girls straight to the hot tub in the suite. Have the bellman bring up a bottle of Mr. Bubble, scented candles, and some stuffed olives. After all, I *am* a working writer on assignment, and the higher-minded types in the paper's editorial department might deem my taking a publicist to a titty bar to be some sort of breach of journalistic ethics. It's unfortunate, but there are still a lot of fucking prudes in this business.

"What did you just say?!!" LapGal hisses. The hostess is taken aback as well. Seems I'd inadvertently fantasized aloud. Been trying to cut back on that.

"I'm not sure," I say, "but do either of you find whatever it was appealing?"

• ♈ ♈ ♈ •

Five fifteen in the morning. I'm alone in my suite. I've got four hours to file a column, which leaves about two hours for a power nap, a trip downstairs for a little gambling, in-room porn, or some good old-fashioned drunken dialing. But, as is often the case in these situations, I pass out while trying to decide. I haven't set the alarm or put in for a wake-up call but I don't need to. There's a job to be done, and no matter how impaired I might get doing research, my internal clock never fails. This is essential to success in my line of work, as is easy access to a toilet and an endless supply of Tylenol. I will wake up in time to compose an essay extolling the virtues of the high-end vodka brand that brought me here to Vegas, and the publicist will forgive me my earlier indiscretion because it's the column she really wants, not me. They all want the column because the column is the pipeline to you, the consumer. I'm merely the conduit. We live in a world where it's unethical to actually pay cash for media coverage; instead they take some guy like me to some place like this and pay the freight. Never mind that this weekend will cost more than I make in a month—that is what is called an "uptown problem." Any enjoyment any of us extract from this little publicity dance is purely ancillary.

But as usual I'm getting ahead of myself. Before I get to the "tell all" about my rather unusual profession, and the rather usual manner in which I practice it, you ought to know how I ended up here in the first place. And that story begins, quite literally, with an accident.

You never forget the first time you learned that the phrase "piss drunk" is not just a colorful figure of speech. For me it came in January 1994, in a small one-bedroom unit on the outskirts of Aspen, Colorado, a town unlike any I'd known before. I'd gone there intending to visit a college friend for a few days on my way to "finding myself" in California, but for a variety of reasons best left to my eventual biographer, I decided to stay a while. In the beginning there were four guys living together in extremely tight quarters. Rent: three hundred dollars each for the two fellas sharing the bedroom, two hundred apiece for the "living room boys"—Joe and me.

It happened after yet another long day of Phase II drinking— Phase I is where you can still count the number of drinks you've had; Phase II is where you just count the *hours* you've been drinking, figuring your burn rate is about six or seven drinks an hour—it's not unlike the drug guys in movies who weigh the money instead of counting it. And it had been a ski season filled with too many Phase IIs. That time, it was Jägermeister and cheap beer slam-dancing in my cranial mosh pit, and I had to go something awful. Unable to move, I opened the floodgates right there on the living room floor, relief mixing with animal shame. Bad enough in any case, but worse then because the living room floor doubled as my bed every other night. On the "other" other night, Joe took the floor. As soon as he found out I'd soiled the carpet, however, Joe rightfully laid full-time claim to the sofa and from then on, the floor was all mine.

In a testament to the fact that Aspen landlords rarely actually visit their property, we didn't get evicted for nearly four months—on Easter Sunday, no less—so I had plenty of time to become quite familiar with my own waste. The last thing I thought of every night before I passed out was urine, and it wasn't the scent of fresh-brewed coffee that roused me each morning. When I finally peeled myself off the floor after another hard night, I put full faith in the Prayer of the Eternally Wasted: "Dear God, please let there be enough cash in my jeans to purchase at least one Bloody Mary."

Despite my pleading and well-constructed appeal to their better natures, the fellas in the bedroom wouldn't clear a space for me in there. Odd jokes were told along the lines of, "This room is mine, that one is urine." They told me they paid extra so that they could have some privacy, and left unspoken that only a fool would allow a bed/floor-wetter into their personal sleeping space. Neither of them had ever brought a woman home, and I often wondered if they might have been lovers. They were brothers, though, so I guess that would have been kinda weird, even by decadent resort standards. Eventually it dawned on me that they didn't want me in their room because they were afraid I'd *do* something to it. Something out of the ordinary, that is. It's a shock to find that even relatively weird people—the sort nowhere near the mainstream—can be worried that one is capable of behavior horrible beyond reason. It's another shock to realize they probably have a point.

Joe and I brought lots of women home—no small feat given that neither of us had any money. We were poor because we didn't have real jobs. In those days I worked twelve hours a week babysitting skis at a slope called Buttermilk Mountain for six dollars an hour and, more important, a free ski pass. Joe was a busboy at a local restaurant and, on occasion, a professional gigolo. The little money we made we spent on alcohol. A *shitload* of alcohol. And we worked the system. There were several joints that offered free happy-hour food, so we survived on that and the surprisingly filling pretzel mix at our favorite dive, Cooper Street Pier. Whenever we weren't skiing—and often when we were—we were drunk. Sometimes we'd be taking drugs, too, because drugs help manage the shakes. Cocaine was more readily available in Aspen than anywhere I'd ever been. The bank machines spit out rolled-up twenties, and when most people said they were doing bumps, they weren't talking about mogul runs.

On one occasion I was driven to wonder aloud why, despite the myriad reasons they shouldn't, women would now and then go home with guys like Joe and me. Kate the bartender said it was because we were ski bums. "Tourists and freshmen* love ski bums," she explained. "They're like trophies. Rites of passage. A notch on their belts."

I didn't know whether to be flattered or offended at being called a bum, so I did what I always do when these sorts of dilemmas arise: I ordered another shot of whiskey. It was 11:45 PM on a Monday, I was still in my ski clothes, and a cute blonde was giving me the eye. I thought, *My God, Kate's right!* Then I opted to invest even more money in recreational pursuits and bought the blonde a **cocktail.**

⚡ The Origin of the Word "Cocktail" ⚡

Truth is, nobody knows for sure where the word "cocktail" came from, but several plausible theories exist. Some etymologists claim cocktail is derived from the French word "coquetier," or "egg cup," the little containers used to serve boiled eggs. In the early 1800s, a New Orleans apothecary named Antoine Peychaud (of Peychaud Bitters fame) invented a drink containing absinthe, brandy, and bitters and served it inside a coquetier. Others contend that the cocktail owes its name to the dubious bygone practice of garnishing mixed drinks with rooster feathers—and you thought bamboo umbrellas were tacky. It is also possible cocktails are so called due to alcohol's capacity to cock one's tail. I'm a cock, after all, and always looking for tail.

I'm of the opinion that cocktail is derived from "cock-ale," a rotgut mixture of ale and minced rooster meat that was all the rage in Jolly Olde England in the seventeenth and eighteenth centuries. Anyone interested in mixing up a batch need only procure a cask of fortified brew, add a sack containing spices and a rooster that's been mashed to a pulp, and allow the mixture to settle for a week. Umm . . . sounds cock-a-doodle-yummy, eh?

---

* Aspenese for "newcomers."

I never "lived" anywhere in the many years I spent in Aspen, at least not in the conventional sense. But I crashed at lots of places. One of 'em burned down, and they had a real nice benefit at Planet Hollywood for everyone who'd lived there. Since I was just freeloading, I never saw any of that cash. I also crashed at the North Star, a run-down motel turned housing complex for employees of the Hotel Jerome, where I made shit money carrying rich people's bags. The North Star would be considered decent digs in most towns, but in Aspen it was the ghetto. At one point I shared a studio apartment with four other guys. Housing five grown men in a three-hundred-square-foot studio was a clear violation of safety regulations, not to mention the Geneva Convention, and in order to avoid detection by the property manager, we always had to keep the windows shut and the blinds closed. It stank like hell in that place, but hey, it was home. Rent: $150 a man.

While living in this arrangement I ran for mayor of Aspen under the Happy Hour Party banner. While no connection was ever proven, it was after my platform called for permanently converting luxury hotel rooms to employee housing that I was fired from the swanky Hotel Jerome and left the friendly funk of the North Star. I'd always leave the places behind, but never the lifestyle. For example, most nights seemed to involve some sort of minor ski-town altercation in or around one of Aspen's many nightclubs (as opposed to Philly-style altercations where you can get seriously fucked up), followed by the nagging thought that maybe I had started it. These doubts were generally fueled by acquaintances who had been at the scene and vouched that I had indeed behaved so obnoxiously that they themselves had wanted to pistol-whip me bloody except they were wearing their good T-shirts.

I'd often slip and fall on the ice after last call, which explained the ever-present welts. If I was with a woman, I'd usually execute a precautionary vomit in the men's room in an effort to avoid any ugly incidents once I got her back to her place. And they say chivalry is dead. Eventually, as Rocky Mountain media trivia experts may recall, the *Aspen Daily News* hired me to write about my hideous existence twice a week. Years later, my editor would disclose that virtually every management meeting had the agenda item, "When are you firing Danny?" He would point out that most people in Aspen on any given night were going to drink too much and try to get laid, and that all the married thirtysomething managers were going to go home early, and that I was the voice of Party Aspen. And he'd tell them my behavior was actually an asset to the paper, despite the boycott and loose talk about restraining orders. Anywhere else in the world, my sort of behavior would warrant dismissal, intervention, and likely even incarceration. Not in Aspen. At least, not in *my* Aspen. In my Aspen, it passed for normal, and if you had the stamina to hold forth on the virtue of casual sex while balancing atop a Cooper Street barstool at closing time, well, good for you.

"That," said my editor, "is exactly the point."

Our merry band's existence centered on skiing, but celebrated a postcollegiate lifestyle that may seem reckless from the outside and looks like a sick and frantic survival trip from the inside—especially as one realizes that the real world does not exactly condone any of it. This became evident from time to time, as did the sort of attention-deficit problems associated with the party life. An example: Shortly after we were evicted from the aforementioned apartment—you

know, the one with the pee-soiled carpet—I ran into the landlady and
we talked. She had asked us to leave rather nicely, citing "countless"
violations of the lease, and we had complied without protest. There
are times when you just know it's best to move on. She even came over
on the day we packed up to wish us well.

"I hope this place was good to you guys . . . even though you did
have too many people living here," she said, recounting one of those
countless violations. She added, "I guess you got some use out of that
sofa bed."

Silence.

We had a fucking *sofa bed?* And to think I spent all those nights
on that stinking floor in my own . . . ah, screw it. Other people might
say they pissed themselves laughing when they heard that. Not me; I
know the downside of such sayings.

Of course, it wasn't all fun and games and piss-soaked carpets
in Aspen. The town was in the midst of an identity crisis in the mid-
1990s. Some locals, mainly business interests, deemed it a world-
class ski resort whose lifeblood was tourists' dollars: a town
constantly struggling to find a competitive edge in an industry that
had been steadily declining since the boom-boom '80s. Others, by
whom I mean both ski bums with access to trust funds and
crunchy-granola types who worked for the forest service, believed it
was still a funky little mountain town willing and able to obviate
overdevelopment and cultural homogenization through political
action or sheer force of will. As a columnist, I was content to survey
the battlefield and fire the occasional shot at the local powers-that-
were. Three days before 1996 began, I did just that.

I had been sunk in a deep depression brought on by the jarring realization that, for the twenty-sixth consecutive year, I'd accomplished nothing of any significance. To make matters worse, by living and writing and starving in Aspen, I had been forced to watch all manner of movers and shakers parade into town with their fancy clothes and big wads of cash, and I was consumed with envy. It was shallow of me, to be sure, but it's easy to turn perverted in the face of obscene wealth. During the height of the ski season the airport was a full-blown circus of private planes, limousines, and big-busted women in furs draped on the arms of their fat-cat sugar daddies. The eclectic mix of freewheeling mavericks who'd migrated there in the '60s and '70s had, for the most part, moved on or gone mad. They'd been replaced by Planet Hollywood, Prada, and, worst of all, prickly dot-commers from Silicon Valley. The few throwbacks who remained were so embittered, having watched the rape and pillage of the town by absentee landowners and nouveau-riche boomers, that they'd been reduced to kicking and screaming about the sad state of affairs like spoiled children.

During the holidays, to supplement my meager newspaper income, I waited tables at a local diner. It was there I suffered the greatest indignity of my short-lived service-industry career. One day a very powerful Hollywood executive and his family were seated in my section, all of them clearly determined to run me into the ground during the lunch rush while stripping me of what little self-esteem remained . . . really, I wasn't cut out for waiting tables. The kids were screaming at me. The wife screamed at me. Somebody called on the exec's cell phone and I think he may have handed it to me so the caller could scream at me. It was about all I could handle, yet somehow I managed to hold it together until it came time to take their dessert order.

"Honey," the exec sneered to his wife—did I mention they were bickering the entire meal?—"the guy is waiting to take your order. Everyone's ordered but you." She was chatting with her daughter, and although she clearly saw me and heard him, she chose not to acknowledge either of us. I offered to come back whenever it was she might be ready, but the exec held up a finger to indicate that I should remain there, pen and pad at the ready.

"Honey," he repeated, with decidedly more urgency, "the guy is waiting!"

Yap, yap, yap.

"He's *waiting*, dammit. Now c'mon!"

With that, she turned toward him, first-degree murder in her eyes. It was clear she loathed this man the way sculptors abhor pigeons and, no doubt, for many of the same reasons. She glanced my way for a moment, just long enough for me to register the utter contempt in which she most assuredly held me and all my kind. Then she returned that frosty gaze to her husband and spat, "Isn't that why they call them *waiters?*" Ouch!

Later that afternoon at the newspaper, still seething from the encounter, I penned a column offering service workers tips for surviving difficult guest-relations situations. Among the not-so-perspicacious nuggets was this: "Whenever you feel you've been mistreated by a paying customer, it is always advisable to avoid direct confrontation and to secretly spit in their food before serving it to them." In retrospect, it wasn't very funny and hardly original. In my defense, I had a very horny gal in town visiting from New Orleans and my libido compelled me to complete the damn column in less than twenty minutes, plus I was angry as all hell. The foofaraw that ensued after the tip appeared in the paper, however, was nothing short of remarkable.

It was my first real experience with the Aspen Magnifier, that supernatural lens that takes anything cute or funny or tragic that happens there and magnifies it by the power of the brand name of "Aspen." It's why companies label products from shitty cars to toilet paper with the A-word. Had everyone left me alone, it would have been a one-day story and never made national headlines. That didn't happen.

The nearly all-powerful Aspen Skiing Company expressed its opprobrium by canceling all their advertising with the *Aspen Daily News*, citing the offensive nature of my column. The local Chamber of Commerce also killed their ads and dispatched a fax to all its members encouraging them to do the same. Many did. KOA Radio—the most listened-to talk radio station in Colorado—dubbed me the "Howard Stern of the Rockies," and the *Denver Post* ran a front-page story about the "war" in Aspen. And, oh, what a war it was. For five straight weeks the newspaper's opinion page was filled with letters of support and condemnation. A reporter from *Time* magazine called to discuss the matter. Secret meetings were held. Imprecations were exacted. Calls for me to be either cudgeled or canonized rose lustily from the citizenry. Aspen's very survival seemed to hang in the balance. In short, the spit had hit the fan.

One side labeled me a no-talent jerk who'd bitten the hand that feeds Aspen by insulting tourists. The manager of the ritzy Little Nell Hotel wrote, "Dan Dunn's recent disgusting article in your paper was the height of arrogance and insensitivity towards those who make it possible for us to enjoy living in this wonderful valley. One hopes, for his sake, that no one with an incurable disease spits in *his* food."

The disenfranchised locals in my camp were equally fiery: "Bless Dan Dunn's twisted heart for really getting the job done in the *Daily News*. For those of you who find his humor tasteless, hey, don't eat it," wrote one supporter.

The whole thing had me walking around a little more crabwise than ever before. Constantly having to look over one's shoulder is no way to live, particularly for someone smoking as much weed as I was back then. After the thing broke, I was beset by a series of hardships: my complimentary ski pass was pulled, I tore cartilage in my knee, and I received word that an old friend from the East Coast had been killed in a car accident. Coincidences? Not a chance. The Ski Overlords of Fantasyland had put the hex on me and I couldn't shake it—even after an emergency visit to New Orleans to celebrate Mardi Gras.

You've gotta understand that Aspen was—and still is—a far cry from places like New York City or L.A., where at least the weirdos *look* weird and it's much easier to distinguish between two-bit dipshits and truly vile scum. Things aren't ever what they seem up there in the clouds, although the inherent inscrutability has little to do with the altitude. In Aspen, evil comes impeccably attired and well mannered, yet it will squash you like a bug under a Range Rover before you can say, "Hey, was that Kenny G?" Power twists people, and makes them do awful things. Think your CEO is a motherfucker at work? You should see him on vacation. There's plenty of truth to the old Irish saying: if you want to know what God thinks of money, just look at the people he gives it to.

A TV crew from ABC's *Good Morning America* came to Aspen not long after the spitting-column incident, and local officials went to great lengths to ensure that the national populace saw only a travel-brochure-ready fool's paradise while they munched their cornflakes. At one point during the broadcast, then-host Joan Lunden remarked, "There are all kinds of things going on in this wonderful little town." How's that for a real pisser?

After Aspen I eventually made my way to Los Angeles, where I spent half a decade living hand to mouth, securing the occasional free-lance writing gig along with numerous loans from my long-suffering parents—who, by the way, still consider me a staggering disappointment. Then one day I stumbled, quite literally, into an old friend who happened to be a big-time newspaper editor. The guy was out on the town with a lady *other* than his wife, and before you could say "extortion" or "another round, please," I found myself in the employ of a large international newspaper chain, writing that dream column I used to ramble on about to bartenders on those long, lonely nights when I'd come down with a case of the "crying drunks."

In the beginning, my expertise was limited to cheap domestic beer and Mad Dog, but I persevered (and made a lot of shit up, too), and "The Imbiber" became a hit. The only hitch is that my jet-setting lifestyle doesn't include much cash. See, it's perfectly ethical for liquor conglomerates to send me a free bottle of wine valued at five thousand dollars or whisk me away on an all-expenses-paid junket to a yacht tour of Scottish distilleries; they just can't offer me any money. That would be wrong. So one of my challenges has been to live high on the hog on a lowly reporter's wage.

An author friend of mine once told me that first chapters are like first dates—you start out wondering what to say and end up wondering if you said too much. So let's begin by establishing the kind of trust that makes a long-term relationship possible. For example, you can trust that I am, above all else, a competent and highly trained professional. It's not just that I've reviewed wine and spirits for the likes of Playboy.com, Metro International Newspapers, the *Los Angeles Times*, and the Lou's House of Booze monthly newsletter, or even that I've parked my ever-widening can on more barstools than a two-time divorcée on a singles cruise. No, you can trust me because I truly believe, along with Oscar Wilde, that "work is the curse of the drinking classes," and that adult beverages consumed in moderation are justification for most of Western culture. Thus I agree with the noted Irish tippler George Bernard Shaw, who once said that "alcohol is the anesthesia by which we endure the operation of life." And as most anyone who grew up in an Irish-Catholic family will attest, the operation in question can take longer than separating conjoined twins.

So there you have my booze bona fides . . . but I do come with some baggage. Hell, there isn't a reputable drinks writer alive who doesn't bear the scars inherent in a life spent in dogged pursuit of dangerous mind-altering compounds found in dark establishments invariably filled with coldhearted thugs and loose women. For example, rum and I had a falling-out a half decade ago—the result of an ugly piña colada–related "incident" at a bar in South Philly during a particularly rowdy celebration following an Eagles victory. Swore off the stuff forever. Of course, I said the same thing about betting on Major League Baseball once, too. Okay, more than once. But whaddaya gonna do? Watch Milwaukee Brewers games just *for fun*?

And I simply must go on record as being unequivocally opposed to the much-ballyhooed abomination known as Low-Carb Beer. Or, as my dear old Uncle Denny likes to call it, Diet Swill. If you're worried about packing on pounds while tippling, drink vodka for heaven's sake. Just leave the beer—real, carbo-loaded brew, the way God intended it—to those of us who think love handles are sexy and consider a paunch hanging over the belt a mark of good character. Besides, why settle for "six-pack abs" when you can have a party-ball belly?

Also, of all the annoying trends that have flourished in recent years (celebrities adopting kids in Third World countries, Bluetooth earpieces, gossip blogs by and for insipid quidnuncs, to name a few), none has been more irritating than the widespread use of alcohol abuse as a cop-out for all manner of deplorable behavior. I've been around a lot of bad drunks in my day and seen some moderate drinkers overindulge and act quite peculiar while under the influence. But I don't care who you are or how much you've had to drink—the intoxicating qualities of alcohol cannot be blamed for the following:

+ Anti-Semitism
+ Pedophilia
+ Homosexuality
+ Recording a Paris Hilton CD

When Hilton's *The Simple Life* costar, Nicole Ritchie, was arrested for driving in the wrong direction on an L.A. freeway in late 2006, she admitted to police that she was higher than the price of real estate in Manhattan. Being hopped-up doesn't excuse horrendous driving, but it is a reasonable explanation for it. However, if Ritchie tried to refute the allegations that she's anorexic by claiming a particularly potent appletini made her forget to eat for the past eighteen months, well . . . you see the point. Booze isn't to blame for an eating disorder any more than it is for Mel Gibson's ranting against Jews, or disgraced Congressman Mark Foley's predatory behavior toward young boys. As for Foley being gay (which has nothing to do with him being a pedophile, by the way), that was established when he was born, not when he started getting loaded.

To be sure, excessive consumption of alcohol is to blame for all sorts of trouble, but to allow it to become the go-to scapegoat for all the world's ills is irresponsible and dangerous. I say we put an end to this passing the buck from here on out. But before we do, I want to apologize in advance for any inaccuracies, typos, or flat-out distortions that may appear in the ensuing pages. In my defense, I was probably pretty liquored-up when I wrote most of this, and I think my editor fancies ridiculously expensive liquor a bit too much.

I'll also confess that I used to be somewhat obsessed with politics, regularly digesting everything and anything having to do with the affairs of government. Now, though, I'm just a dabbler. I hear things, and I think about them sometimes, but I no longer think *real hard* about politics. These days my thoughts tend to be more arbitrary. For instance, just last weekend I spent nearly two hours pondering the historical significance of Milton Bradley's Operation—a tabletop game, wildly popular in the late 1970s, that delivers an electric shock to small children with poor hand-eye coordination. Surely, millions of people spanning generations suffered irreparable psychological damage because their parents weren't satisfied with Monopoly. How did Operation pass government safety standards? More important, is it still around?

Now, instead of thinking about politics, I find myself getting drunk a lot and thinking about things like the statue of *David*. That divine masterpiece is worthy of more attention than George W. Bush's failed fiscal and foreign policies. Michelangelo completed *David* in 1504 when he was but twenty-five years old, an age at which most people are still stealing ink-jet cartridges from our employers so we can send badly written Christmas newsletters to people who don't like us anyway. *David* stands today as a reminder of how beautiful we can be, particularly if we manage to be immortalized in marble by Michelangelo. Unfortunately, Michelangelo . . . he dead.

What I'm trying to impress upon you here with this opening salvo is that at the end of the day—a time we call Happy Hour—it's all about developing a solid foundation upon which to build a respectable drinking life. For instance, if the words "White Russian" remind you of Tony's former mistress on *The Sopranos* or a certain dancer who played a love interest on *Sex and The City*, then clearly you need to wean yourself *off* the DVD collections of dearly departed HBO series and haul your couch-potato self down to the local bar. For me, the White Russian has always been on the sophisticated drinks list, even back when I considered it a semi-chick "pace drink" between whiskeys. And it had the huge added advantage of being one of the few cocktails that I could remember the name of and make at home.

Actual date conversation, circa 2005:

"So, babe, welcome to my place. Would you like a drink?"

"Yeah, great . . . how about a Cosmo Double-Twist dismount martini, but with vodka instead of gin and replace the cherry with a kosher olive?"

"Uhhhh, I was thinking this would be a great night for a White Russian."

"Wow. You *are* sophisticated."

Back then, all it took was two ounces of vodka, an ounce or so of Kahlúa, some light cream from the nearby 7-11, and it was James Bondage time. These days—and I suspect this started with the Starbucks crowd—the big thing is the "skinny" White Russian, which includes the same vodka and Kahlúa but topped with soy milk. This was made officially trendy a while back when *USA Today* reported that Jennifer Garner and Molly Simms were among the celebs sipping the SWR, thus removing any question about that paper's dedication to serious investigative journalism.

As you've probably figured out by now, I think it's best we don't get too serious about *anything* here. While I certainly look forward to sharing my thoughts with you on cocktails and drinking in the ensuing pages, I realized something as I typed in the quote from the Irish guy they named the huge dog after: it could be that everything worth thinking about the matter has already been thunk.

Take the late, great comedian and *Hollywood Squares* all-star George Gobel, who swore he'd never been drunk, but maintained he'd often been overserved. Jack Benny's sidekick, Phil Harris, made no apologies, and on more than one occasion claimed he couldn't die until the government found a safe place to bury his liver. So here's a toast to Phil, who passed away in 1995 and is surely enjoying a heavenly martini from time to time: may what goes down not come back up again.

Henny Youngman once said that when he read about the evils of drinking, he gave up reading, and Dylan Thomas defined an alcoholic as "someone you don't like who drinks as much as you do." My all-time favorite tippler-quote comes courtesy of that legendary statesman and fellow Philadelphian Ben Franklin, who cited beer as "proof that God loves us and wants us to be happy."

Benny, I couldn't have put it better myself.

Step 2

When They Say, "You'll Need Shots" to Go to Some Countries, They Don't Mean the Kind at the Airport Bar

Blond, blotto, and broken down in Piccadilly Circus—it marked a rather inglorious end to what had been an otherwise triumphant march across the European continent on the mother of all booze junkets. It was in the summer sometime in the early part of this century, if booze-addled memory serves (and it often doesn't)—the summer I came into my own as a worldly-wise professional wino on my first professional trip abroad. In addition to stops at numerous distilleries, my travels included unexpected encounters with:

- a B-list American actor in Turin
- a tight squeeze involving a chatty Irish gal
- a controversial dessert selection and a pair of Italian-made jeans
- my own personal D-Day on Normandy's Omaha Beach
- a clash with a bungling French airline
- a sighting of the Clash's Mick Jones in London's Trafalgar Square.

You have your business trips. I'll have mine.

'Twas truly a rollicking ride, my sightseeing, spirits-swilling sojourn across the pond. And I did it all on the company dime and as the guest of a series of multinational, junket-sponsoring liquor companies that seldom suspected I was even on vacation. Yet there's no need to fret over missing a single moment because, frankly, many of the moments were excruciatingly dull. The exciting times, though— well, those I preserved in my handy drinking diary. Right, then. Some highlights:

Piccadilly Circus, London. 5:14 PM, Friday, July 21.

Spent the morning in a small pub on the Strand attempting to corner the market on **Guinness.** Pissed the hell out of the Limey bartender by continuously asking him if he "spoke American." You're

ϟ Interview with a Guinness Brewmaster ϟ

In 1759 an enterprising lad named Arthur Guinness negotiated a nine-thousand-year lease (at seventy dollars a year) on the St. James Gate Brewery in Dublin. Guess ole Arthur had a hunch his brew would be around for a while. These days the responsibility for carrying on Arthur's legacy lies with Fergal Murray, who's been head brewmaster at Guinness since 1995. I sat down with him once, and gave him a grilling worthy of Mike Wallace.*

There's a perception in America that Guinness is fattening, when in fact it has fewer calories (about 125 per serving) than most domestic and imported light beers.
FERGAL MURRAY: We've always had the beer this way. Other folks have adapted their beers to appeal to light beer drinkers in the United States, but our beer has always been that way.

continued on next page >>

* a developmentally challenged guy from my old neighborhood, *not* the dude from *60 Minutes*

sure Bill Clinton went to college near here? Noon found me not far from this renowned district of commerce in a terrible wrestling match with powerful demons spawned from the wretched loins of the Guinness beast. As one might expect, the demons scored a decisive victory. Somewhat impaired and quite possibly in need of medical attention, I instead sought refuge in—of all places—a trendy Soho hair salon, under the supervision of an undernourished gay stylist named Lincoln.

I'd be proud of my position as an international degenerate except that, as I'm making this diary entry, at yet another pub, I'm seeking important local travel insight by flipping through the pages of *Reach for the Ground.* This excellent book chronicles the downhill struggle of a true degenerate, an English legend in fact: the late, great *Spectator* columnist Jeffrey Bernard, who served as patron

Does the Guinness available in the States have less alcohol than in Ireland?
It's 4.2 percent alcohol in the States—exactly the same as we drink in Dublin and the rest of Western Europe.
What type of food goes well with Guinness?
My favorite is seafood with pints of stout. Then again, there's nothing better than a cottage pie or an Irish stew with Guinness. Also, fusion foods—Asian fusion, especially. And it goes great with salads with bacon on top, too.
So, basically, Guinness pairs well with everything but nachos?
It goes great with nachos!
We're all blissfully obsessed with celebrities. Do famous people drink Guinness?
Any of the leading actors of the world, when they come to Dublin, they enjoy a pint. The Rolling Stones are big fans. U2, of course. I've seen George Clooney having a pint, and Pierce Brosnan, too. But a lot of the girls drink it—Angelina Jolie is a big fan.
And I'm a big fan of Angelina . . . you, too?
Oh, yes.

saint and hero to crapulous types the world over.* Well-deserved regards to former *GQ* magazine Mixology columnist Terry Sullivan for recommending Bernard's fine work, said recommendation coming on the heels of a similar steering toward J. P. Donleavy's debased *The Ginger Man*† and a brilliant piece of madness called *Killoyle* penned by a psychotic alcoholic by the name of Boylan. There's a trend here.

Cheers, Sullivan, ole boy . . . the irreparable damage to my Rube Goldbergian psyche is now complete. You'll hear from my solicitors. And it should be noted that I also have blond hair now. Really, I do. I don't know how I feel about the new look, but Soho seems cool, and Lincoln assured me I look like the tits!

Turin Palace Hotel, Turin, Italy. Late at Night, Wednesday, July 5.

I never had any reason to hate the French until today. I arrived in Milan much earlier this morning after connecting in Paris on Air France.° My luggage was lost, and because I understood about as much French as the average Pentecostal preacher from Alabama, it was impossible to ascertain whether anyone at the airline had the

---

* Bernard, who died of renal failure in 1997, was immortalized in Keith Waterhouse's hit West End play, *Jeffrey Bernard Is Unwell*, starring Peter O'Toole. The play's title refers to the one-line apology the *Spectator* would publish whenever Bernard was either too drunk or hungover to produce his regular column.

† *The Ginger Man* is the twisted tale of a wretched drunkard, and should be required reading for all junior high school students, moralists, and rock singers. It's worth reading for the sheep's-head scene alone, which everybody who ever spent $32.50 for a slice of foie gras ought to revisit to get their priorities straight.

° Motto: "We love to fly . . . and our planes smell like armpits!"

faintest clue as to where my things might be. An Air France representative offered me a lengthy clarification in her native tongue. Not a
single word was recognizable, but fearing the repercussions of being
perceived as an ignorant American pig-dog, I cleverly sprinkled the
"conversation" with a liberal helping of "oui," which I understand is
French for, "Due to a lack of understanding, I have to pee." My luggage, I think they assured me, would no doubt arrive within the hour.
So here I am, dining naked and alone in my room. I tried to have a
meal at the hotel restaurant, but they didn't allow sweatpants, and
that's all I had, thanks to Air France.* The sweatpants, incidentally,
were hanging from my hotel window; this in hopes of airing out the
considerable odor of eau de armpit.

While checking in, I bumped into the American actor Giovanni
Ribisi, a cat I'd met before at press junkets and through mutual
friends. Turns out that Vanni, as he's known around Hollywood, was
shooting a movie in Turin. He graciously pretended to remember
me, so in return I made no reference to his involvement in the horrendous remake of *The Mod Squad*. Our encounter played out something like this:

Int. Italian Hotel Lobby—Day

DAN, a strikingly handsome travel journalist attired in stylish, if
slightly gamey, sweatpants, is standing next to the American actor
GIOVANNI RIBISI, who starred in *Saving Private Ryan*, *The Boiler
Room*, and *The Mod* . . . er, never mind.

---

* Travel Tip #102: When traveling great distances, style should always take a backseat to comfort.

DAN: Hey, Vanni, how's it going?

Giovanni feigns recognition.

GIOVANNI: Hey, um . . . my friend-a, it's-a going okay-a.

DAN: (looking more strikingly handsome with each passing moment, wearing sweats like few in the business) Great. Great. Funny seeing you here.

GIOVANNI: Yes-a. I'm-a—how you say?—en-joy-ing-a my time-a here in Torino.

DAN: Why are you talking like that, dude?

GIOVANNI: Scusee, but-a have-a been-a studying-a Italiano for several months-a, and I must-a stay-a in character-a.

DAN: Several months. Really?

GIOVANNI: Yes-a.

DAN produces a notepad from his jacket pocket and scribbles something. EXTREME CLOSE-UP on what he's written: "His dialect coach used to work for Air France Communications. . . . I predict another *Mod Squad.*"

Ristorante Del Cambio, Turin, Italy. Thursday, July 6.

Built in 1757 to the design of famed architect Antonio Bellino, Del Cambio is a marvel. Located across from the Palazzo Carignano—home of the first Italian Parliament—this place has long been *the* spot for the biggest names in Italian politics . . . not that I purport to know the names of many Italian politicians, living or dead, given that they've had forty-six governments since World War II. I am, however, familiar with the legend of Count Cavour, who is credited with unifying Italy. They say Cavour spoke Italian, thought in French, and dined Piedmontese-style at Del Cambio, his "very favorite restaurant in all the world," according to the headwaiter.

Sitting among a group of very excellent people—Europeans and Americans alike—in a luxurious dining room bearing the count's name, directly beneath a bronze plaque emblazoned with tricolor ribbons commemorating the count's favorite place to sit, eating food and drinking wine fit for . . . well, for Count fucking Cavour, it stands to reason I'd be merrier than the bald guy on *The Mary Tyler Moore Show*. But I'm not. On the contrary, I'm quite troubled. And today, being fully in touch with my previously latent Franco-enmity, I lay all the blame for my disquietude on the French, a people whose largest air carrier has yet to recover my lost baggage. Hence the Italian jeans.

If you gave a pair of Italian-made men's jeans a passing glance, you'd likely presume them to be—as I did—much like America's own Levi's or Gap denims or something from the good rack at TJ Maxx. Same color, same feel, same bloated price tag (except at TJ Maxx). You might even grab a pair in your usual size off the rack—as I did— and purchase them sans fitting. This would be a mistake. In the interest of consumer safety, I now present:

TRAVEL TIP #31: Never purchase Italian-made men's jeans without first trying them on. Italian-made men's jeans are made for unusually thin males devoid of hips or testicles. If you have hips and/or testicles, it's advisable to avoid Italian jeans altogether.

If, however, you find yourself in a situation where, for instance, an inept French airline has carelessly lost most of your clothing, and a

new pair of Italian-made jeans is the only affordable alternative to a
pair of fetid sweatpants, I suggest trying on a pair at least three sizes
larger than normal.

"Aren't those jeans just squeezing the hell out of your balls?"
asked the woman sitting next to me—a nice Irish gal who, it turns
out, worked for Bacardi.

"Huh?" I mumbled, shifting uneasily and wondering how it could
be so obvious.

"I said, aren't you just having *a hell of a ball?* I am. I really, really am."

She smiled, and I smiled back at her. When she turned away, I
winced: the eggplant ravioli with fresh tomato and wild mushrooms
had gone straight to my hips and I feared my Italian-made jeans
might explode.

Then the count arrived. Not the dead one, but a quite animated
latter-day version. Count Esconsio is a bigwig with Martini & Rossi,
which is owned by Bacardi, the company hosting the International
Bartenders Competition. The IBC was the reason I was in Turin.
Bacardi had invited me to attend, as they somehow got the impression
I was an important member of the American media. Had they known
I was barely employed and researching my new book, *Why Air France
Fucking Sucks*, instead of their latest sparkling wine or the IBC, it was
unlikely I'd have been in that restaurant wearing those Italian jeans.
Esconsio proved to be a cool cat. Rich. Educated. Dashing. Italian. He
had a way of making the guests feel so special that few even noticed
that he treated the help like garbage. Dessert was the most beautifully
prepared dish I'd ever seen: a large yellowish gelatin mold with vibrant
red and blue wild berries suspended inside. I stared at my dessert

plate, admiring it. I even took a picture of it. Count Esconsio, however, was unimpressed. He lifted his plate, eyeing the quivering gelatin
mold suspiciously. After a long while in which he seemed to be con-
templating some sort of hate crime, the count snapped his fingers
angrily. The headwaiter quickly materialized at the table. Esconsio
was unhappy.

"What is this . . . *trembling cake?*"

The headwaiter bowed his head in humiliation. His face turned
the same shade of red I imagined my poor balls to be.

"Turin is home to some of the finest chocolates in the world,"
Esconsio continued, "and you give my guests this . . . this . . . this *trembling cake.*"

A tear rolled down the headwaiter's cheek.

"TAKE IT AWAY!!!" Esconsio barked.

Suddenly, the headwaiter collapsed under the weight of his
shame; another powerful reminder that the service industry isn't for
the faint of heart . . . in any language.

Sandwich Shop, Viareggio, Italy. Sunday, July 9.

My friend and co-perambulater on this European sojourn was famed
Phoenix deejay Dead Air Dave,* a fascinating fella with the right connections and a solid rep who nonetheless always seems to be "between

---

* Dead Air Dave hails from his mother's womb. He has been a radio-industry professional
for more than twenty-five years, but really stays in the business only to meet chicks who
would otherwise not give him a second glance. He is the author of the not-likely-to-be-
published book *How to Turn Spite into a Cottage Industry.* Dave continues to struggle with his
arrested development at his home in Arizona.

gigs." Despite hovering in a perpetual state of underemployment, Dave's got a boatload of money, and he's more than willing to share so long as I avoid inquiries into the source of his wealth and the contents of the fortified underground bunker in his backyard.

Over the years, Dead Air has become my road-trip go-to guy whenever a wingman/scapegoat is necessary. He and I left Turin this morning following a confrontation ignited by our vehicle, a 1966 Morris Mini Cooper S, provided gratis for the duration of our stay by some PR flak from Mini's corporate parent, BMW.

BMW gave me the car to drive across Europe because, like the people at Bacardi, they were somehow under the impression that I was an important member of the American media. Had they known I was barely employed and writing about my balls and nonstop drunkenness instead of their automobile, it's entirely likely I'd be hitchhiking my way to London. Now to the encounter . . .

We were waiting at a traffic light on our way out of Turin when a black-toothed young Italian lad armed with a squeegee and a spray bottle filled with a turbid liquid approached the car. He smelled as if he'd been flying for days aboard an Air France jet.

"No, no," I shouted as he began spraying his gray splooge all over the Mini's little windshield. "No money! We have no money to give you."

He took a step back and glowered at me. Then he seemed to notice our Mini's most distinctive feature—its roof. Being among the most famous of all British motorcars, and this particular vehicle being a demo for the media, the folks at BMW/Mini had gone ahead and proudly slapped a Union Jack across the roof—painted it across the entire top of the car, like a big bulls-eye. You see, not everyone in Europe is as fond of the British as the British seem to be of themselves—most notably the French (who aren't fond of anyone) and the Italians (especially, it turns out, homeless, black-toothed Italians).

"Oh," he sneered brokenly—or perhaps "oh" is also part of the Italian vernacular—"you are Eeeeenglish."

"Well, actually . . ."

"You are Eeeeenglish," he re-sneered, "so that makes you a neeeeger." He flipped us off and marched away.

I turned and said to Dave: "Did he just call me a neeeeger?"

"I believe so," Dave replied.

"Wow, my first racial slur. I feel elated."

And just like that, I'd been inducted into the brotherhood . . . by an Italian, of all people. I made a note to reconsider the rap career.

Near a Tower that Is about to Fall Over in Pisa, Italy. Later the Same Day.

There's a game I like to play back home called "Paying Wrong," and it really is a hoot. It works like this: you must play in a convenience store or some other comparable establishment where you're not in danger of discovering Harvard-trained employees behind the counter. If you owe $8.50, for example, give the clerk $12 and watch his cranial abacus immediately start to malfunction. The bill comes to $19.25? Hand the guy a $20 and three $1 bills and observe as he desperately tries to determine what sort of strange change combination you might be after.

Usually, the dupe in your game of Paying Wrong will spend a few moments doing calculations while you chortle mischievously to yourself—and this becomes even more entertaining if there happens to be a line of impatient customers queued up behind you, adding to the clerk's pressure. In most cases, they'll eventually give you correct change, assuming you simply made a mistake. The thrill of the Paying Wrong game, however, comes in the possibility that you'll be confronted by an incensed counterperson who demands to know why you forked over $31 to settle a $28.79 tab. At that point—by rule—you must admit that you deliberately paid wrong simply to get a rise out of the clerk. If you're tossed from the store without the goods, you lose. If the clerk takes a swing at you, you win. Again, you have your business trips, and I'll have mine. And that brings us to . . .

TRAVEL TIP #2: Avoid Paying Wrong in foreign countries in which you have little or no grasp of the language, because in all likelihood you will lose . . . or win . . . or both.

An example: the cost of my Leaning Tower of Pisa ceramic night-light was four euros—approximately five dollars. Erroneously thinking it would be a gas to pay wrong in another country, I gave the clerk seven euros and waited for the confusion to set in. He promptly handed me one euro in change and moved on to the next customer.

"Wait," I stammered. "This isn't the correct change."

A blank stare. What I said hadn't registered. As Americans are wont to do when confronted with a language barrier, I began speaking in a slow staccato, dropping modifiers, and employing a bad accent that would have made Vanni damn proud: "Change-a. Not-a. Correct-a."

The clerk eyed me with curiosity, in much the same way one might observe monkeys at the zoo. Then another clerk intervened.

"Whassa da problem?" he asked.

"Oh, good, you speak-a Inglesias . . . um, this night-light"—I sheepishly held up the object of contention—"she cost-a four euro, correct-a?"

"Cie."

"Right, right," I continued. "Well, I gave him seven euros, and he gave me only one euro in return." Both clerks were now examining the monkey cage. "Seven! I gave him *seven* euros."

Ooo-oo-ah-ah-ee-ee . . .

"Scusee, sir, but why you give seven euro when it cost only four euro?"

"Because I was paying wrong."

"Paying wrong?"

"Yes!"

I was now jumping up and down inside the cage, banana in one hand, swollen red balls in the other, risking being mistaken for an Air France baggage handler.

"What is this . . . this *paying wrong?*"

"Paying wrong is . . . um, it's . . . oh, forget it!"

Ooo-oo-ah-ah-ee-ee . . .

One other note from Pisa: anyone meaning to study architecture in Italy should cancel their plans ASAP—these clowns are obvious hacks. The tower in Pisa wears more support than Dolly Parton, held up as it is by a huge steel girdle, a ceramic corset, and cables while engineers excavate the ground beneath it in the hope of leveling the foundation. Not a chance. Mark my words, this structure will topple within the next ten years. The tower—which took nearly two hundred years to complete—began leaning in 1178, just five years after construction began. This begs the obvious question: why the hell did they keep building the damn thing? They could have cut it off at the first or second level and wound up with, at worst, a much less embarrassing "Leaning Rotunda of Pisa." But part of the joy of travel is finding out that other cultures are just as screwed up as Back Home. And this tower left me heading for the Mini just a bit less culturally humiliated by that "World's Largest Groundhog" shit on I-70 in Kansas.

The Sporting Club, Nice, France. Friday, 1:00 PM.

I was reading a book called *We Wish to Inform You that Tomorrow We Will Be Killed with Our Families*, an account of the genocide that occurred in Rwanda in 1994 after the Rwandan government implemented a policy that called on everyone in the Hutu majority to murder everyone in the Tutsi minority. The low-tech massacres—largely by machete—were carried out at dazzling speed, and eight hundred thousand Tutsis and Tutsi sympathizers were killed in a hundred days. Pastors in one Tutsi community sent a letter to their church president, a Hutu, that included the chilling phrase that gave author Philip Gourevitch his title. Principally, the Hutu leadership in Kigali cultivated the Hutu Power frenzy that drove Rwandans to kill their neighbors, but they had some outside help in carrying out the genocide. It turns out that almost all of the Rwandan government's military and financial support before, during, and after the massacres was provided by one European country. That country was the very one in which I now found myself sunning: France. So I was sitting there on the beach imagining myself surrounded by dead Rwandans, and adding one more item to my list of reasons to hate the French. Not that they cared, because they clearly hated me more.

I looked down at the hideous French-made purple corduroy shorts I had been compelled to purchase because—in case you missed it—France's largest airline had lost and had yet to recover my luggage in Italy. A fat yellow-toothed local with grotesque saggy bare tits was sitting next to me smoking incessantly and yapping away to an even fatter and froggier confrère—no doubt making fun of my fashion misfortune.

Ohhh, my kingdom for the fall of France.

Then Chloe, a regular Venus de Milo in a miniskirt and with a serving tray, appeared in all her sensualistic splendor. "Would you like another beer, monsieur?" she purred.

"I don't believe 'like' really covers the bill on my affinity for beer, Chloe," I replied suavely.

She giggled, flashed a kittenish smile, then bumped and grinded her way to the bar. Seconds later she returned with an ice-cold Kronenbourg.* Hey, maybe the French aren't so bad after all. To American men, French women turn out to be very much akin to their language—sexy as hell, but hard to pick up. Dead Air Dave wasn't having much luck with the women or the language. Dave leered lasciviously at Chloe

---

* Kronenbourg is the leading beer brand in France, which is sort of like being the valedictorian at summer school.

after she handed him a beer, and the repugnance on her face was as palpable as the contemptuous quiver of her ample bosom.

"Mer-soir," Dave told her, which translates roughly to, "Thank evening."

"I think you meant *merci*," I corrected Dave after Chloe left. He shot me a funny look. He'd been perverting languages since we arrived in Italy, and he damn sure wasn't going to stop in France. In fact, Dave had butchered the Italian language with such consistency and conviction that many of the Italians we met along the way had begun sprinkling their own conversations with "Dead Air-isms." I damn near spit out a mouthful of trembling cake in that restaurant in Turin when the oh-so-Italian Count Esconcio, lord of the Martini & Rossi family, made reference to "Florenze"—a Dead Air-ism combining the English and Italian words for the country's cultural center. Rather than exhibit embarrassment over his linguistic lapse, the count seemed downright tickled to be playing the role of the ill-adapted American.

"I like-a the way-a dat sounds-a," he had chuckled to Dave. "I'm-a gonna go to America and be-a talking like you soon—how you say?—getting *jeeegy* with it." Then he raised a toast to Dead Air Dave and America, and all the Italians lit up like Roman candles. My God . . . what are we doing to these people and their culture? First the Big Mac and Air Jordan and now this? Before you know it, the statue of *David* will be on display on the state-fair circuit in Missouri wearing hideous purple shorts.

In Italian, when someone thanks you—*grazie*—it's appropriate to respond "*prego*," which means "you're welcome." Dead Air's first attempt at "you're welcome" came out "primo," and he stuck with it.

"But Dave, 'primo' means 'great,'" I told him.

"Really?" he replied, thoughtfully stroking the bushy soul patch beneath his lower lip. "Well, it's better to be great than merely to be welcome, eh?"

He had a point. A primo point, actually.

I was having my own fun with language—namely, learning and utilizing insulting French phrases. My favorites so far:

"*Vos enfants sont très beaux. Ils sont adoptés?*" ("Your children are very attractive. Are they adopted?") First used this one the day before on an obnoxious couple from Calais who were causing quite a disturbance in the lobby at Nice's Hotel Splendid, which is anything but. We were paying 250 euros a night for a broom closet sans windows, sleeping on wooden racks that the Plantagenets no doubt had used to torture the Capetians back in the Hundred Years' War (I'd been reading a lot). In retaliation, I phoned the front desk regularly and at the top of my lungs complained, "*J'ai une grenouille dans mon bidet!*" ("I have a frog in my bidet!") demanding it be removed immediately. Then I dropped a postcard bearing Victor Hugo's likeness into the bidet and left the room. I was informed the entire housekeeping staff threatened to quit if called upon to visit my broom closet again.

"*Est-ce que vous êtes ivre?*" ("Are you drunk?") I kept posing this question to Dave, to which he invariably replied, "mer-soir."

And I had a real zinger at the ready for my departure from France. When the customs agent asked if I had anything to declare, I planned to respond, "*Juste mon genie.*" ("Only my genius.") Much thanks to the late, great Oscar Wilde for that one.

Quarter Ancien, Cognac, France. Wendesday? Thursday? Hard to Tell.

No respectable spirits writer would chronicle a monthlong European vacation without including some functional content for tax-write-off purposes. A caveat: on the day I decided to do this research, I wound up getting shittier than Ted Kennedy on holiday in Nantucket and therefore cannot reasonably be held responsible for the validity of the following information.

In the heart of the Charente region of western France, the locals refer to the unique climate and soils, and the proximity of the ocean, as a "happy accident of nature." And just why are they so elated? Because the climate and soil, along with moisture from the sea, are key factors in the production of cognac—that most delicious and stately of libations. Cognac is a versatile spirit that can be enjoyed neat or with water as a *digestif** or an *aperitif.*† It's also nice on the rocks or in a cocktail or slugged straight from the bottle while muttering obscure French insults. In the short time Dave and I had been in Cognac, we enjoyed it seventeen ways from Sunday . . . wait, is today Sunday? And did I mention cognac goes well over cold cereal?

Unlike beer, cocktails, or divorce attorneys, picking a cognac requires a bit more thought and effort than it takes to utter the words, "A tall, cold one, please." One of the keys to ordering cognac is understanding the label. Cognac is a product with a controlled appellation, with certificates of age and origin issued by the industry's governing

---

* An after-dinner drink

† A before-dinner drink

body. No cognac may be sold unless it is at least two and a half years old. The minimum age of the youngest *eau-de-vie* (spirit) used in the blend determines the name under which the cognac will be sold. And that brings us to the aforementioned know-how—the degrees of cognac:

- VS (or Three Stars)—the youngest *eau-de-vie* is less than four and a half years old.
- VSOP (Very Superior Old Pale) or VO (Very Old)—the youngest *eau-de-vie* is between four and a half and six and a half years old.
- Napoleon, XO, Extra, Hors D'Age—the youngest *eau-de-vie* is more than six and a half years old.

Pretty impressive, eh? Lest you think I'm getting too serious about my career as a spirits journalist, I must confess that I copied the above information verbatim off a placard in a pisser. Not that I'm a complete hack, mind you. I was in Europe on assignment for a prominent international newspaper conglomerate and I had every intention of returning stateside with award-caliber material. Truth is, I was heavily into some serious research on the most celebrated spirit of the region. Earlier that day, Dead Air Dave and I stormed into the Hennessy factory without an appointment, which is really the only way to effectively storm any building. After flashing spurious credentials, we demanded to be given abundant samples of the finest cognac in stock. Amazingly, they complied, as did the people across the street at Otard Cognac. And Rémy Martin. And Hine.

"What is this stuff here we've been drinking?" Dave asked, admiring a nearly empty bottle of sweet brown liquid.

"That, my friend, is the nectar of the gods," came the reply.

Billed as the world's rarest cognac, Richard Hennessy is the standard by which to judge all others. Created as a tribute to the founder of Hennessy, some of the cognacs in the blend date back to the early 1800s. The result is elegant, complex, and refined, with a rich bouquet that reveals a succession of aromas that have evolved over time: vanilla, spices, pepper, and delicately scented flowers. Tasting reveals nuances of ripe fruit, the finesse of oak, and other complex flavors. And as if the taste weren't impressive enough, Richard Hennessy is cradled in an exquisitely designed handblown crystal decanter from the Cristallerie Royale de Saint Louis. Each bottle is cushioned in a satin-lined nubuck presentation case and includes an informational book containing the individual bottle number and Maurice Hennessy's signature, confirming its authenticity. Of course, the best doesn't come cheap. A bottle retails for $2,500, and a snifter in a restaurant or bar should set you back at least $200.

"What are you doing?" Dave asked as I transferred the contents of a relatively inexpensive bottle of Otard cognac into the empty Richard Hennessy bottle.

"I can probably get a thousand bucks easy for this on eBay," I told him. "All I need is some glue to reseal this baby."

Dave eyed me skeptically. "It doesn't seem right, man."

"Neither does reality television, but it's apparently here to stay," I shot back.

And I've got an appropriate appellation for the ersatz Richard

Hennessy, something the dupe I sell it to will likely utter after he realizes he's been had: U.S.O.B.

Omaha Beach, Normandy, France. 5:30 PM, Saturday.

Well over half a century ago, Allied troops stormed the beaches of northern France and emerged victorious in what proved to be a series of the most devastating battles in the history of modern warfare. Many Allied soldiers gave their lives on those beaches to defeat Hitler's Nazis, making it possible in this new millennium for me to roam freely across the rolling green hills and immense sand bunkers of Normandy with my fellow man—in this case, Dead Air Dave—and to joyously proclaim, "Man, I just hit the shit out of that five-iron!"

Yes, proving beyond a shadow of a doubt that nothing is sacred, some scum-sucking greedhead greased the corrupt local zoning board a few years back and got permission to build a golf course just a chip shot away from the site of the most historic battles of World War II. Remember the gruesome depiction of the D-Day invasion at the outset of Steven Spielberg's epic *Saving Private Ryan?* Turned your stomach, didn't it? Now think about all those young GIs paying the ultimate price in blood so that rich white guys could desecrate the ground with putters and sand wedges. You can't miss it if you try. The road to the American Cemetery at Normandy is littered with billboards exhorting visitors to "Golf Omaha Beach." When I first saw one, it was damn near all I could take. And my initial disgust gave way to all-out fury when I learned that golf carts weren't included in the exorbitant greens fees.

Now, believe me, by no means am I trying to belittle the sacrifice my grandparents' generation made at Normandy, but when it comes to golf, it's all about impressing other people with the courses you've played. You think guys fork over four hundred and fifty dollars to play Pebble Beach because they enjoy duffing balls into the ocean? Of course not. They pay to play there so that for the rest of their lives they can tell less fortunate hackers that they played the most picturesque course in America. And tell me, how many golfers *you* know have played Omaha Beach?

I rest my case.

Arromonche, a Few Miles North of Omaha Beach. Later the Same Day.

We found ourselves tipping a few beers with a group of American World War II veterans making their first visit to Normandy since the D-Day invasion. Rather than being somber and forlorn, as you might expect, these guys were quite ebullient: seems time really does heal all wounds.

"This place is beautiful," said a man with a big, furry white mustache, "although I don't remember it being that way back then." His remark was met with a chorus of "hear, hear" and the clink of toasting beer mugs.

"Hard to believe what went on down on those beaches," added another.

"Hear, hear!!!"

"It's a damn miracle we all made it out alive," said yet another.

More hear, hears and mug-clinking.

"Yep, a goddamn miracle."

Emphatic hear-hearing and clinking.

"I remember being dug in near the water with bullets whizzing overhead thinking I was going to be stuck in that bunker forever," added the man with the furry mustache.

"Tell me about it," I mumbled with disgust.

Silence.

Then greater silence.

Followed by absolutely no sound whatsoever.

"Well," I finally chortled nervously, "I got caught in a bunker on the eighth at Omaha Beach and wound up making triple-bogey on the hole. And you guys thought *you* had it tough out there!"*

Piccadilly Circus, London. Very Late, Friday.

So as you can see, it was truly a tumultuous ride across the European continent. After several rounds of drink—on Yours Truly, of course—the old American GIs at Arromonche forgave me, chalking my seeming disrespect up to innocent precociousness. But it was really my usual nervous reaction to something actually significant. Sometimes we use humor to deal with what we can't understand, and sometimes we use it to deal with things that we understand perfectly damn well.†

By midnight at Arromonche, I knew all the words to "The Battle Hymn of the Republic" and was made an honorary member of the 58th Armored Division. From Normandy, Dead Air and I headed

---

* Insert rimshot here.

† Told you I was reading a lot.

north and spent several uneventful yet extremely relaxing days at the beachfront hamlet of Etretat as guests of the Benedictine company. We crossed the English Channel in the Mini via the Eurotunnel (take *that*, Air France!) and arrived in London in time to catch one of my all-time-favorite musical heroes, Mick Jones of the Clash, walking a little dog across Trafalgar Square.

Should I stay or should I go?

Go, I suppose.

So it was back to the States for a respite, then off to the jungles of Malaysia to cover some adventure race sponsored by Tiger Beer. Maybe I'd whip up a multipart series for the paper on the heels of that great passage, assuming snakes, orangutans, or the indigenes didn't do me in. Until we meet again, Europe, I noted, keep reaching for the ground.

Step 3

Whisky: Proudly Destroying Livers Since 1088

As you might have guessed, some of this chapter will have something to do with "whisky," as it's spelled in Scotland, along with "whiskey," the stuff they produce pretty much everywhere else. Do the Scots have "E-ness envy?" We'll evaluate. But before we get to that, I'd like to introduce you to my roommate in Los Angeles, who'll be playing the role of antagonist in this tome. He has a real name, but for as long as I've known him* I've been calling him "Bottomfeeder," after a song by my friend Steve Skinner. And, for the record, Bottomfeeder isn't sure this book of mine is such a good idea. Of course, he's never been much of a fan of the written word—mine or anyone else's.

"All of us learn to write in the second grade," he told me. "Most of us go on to greater things."

"Interesting point," I replied. "Who said that?"

"I did," he said. "Quote me."†

---

* We were "introduced" shortly before I went on the big European junket you just read about.

† Hall of Fame basketball coach Bobby Knight said it first.

Then he polished off another of my **Grolschs**, lit up a Pall Mall he'd shoplifted from a convenience store, and began frantically searching for the TV remote as though there were a cigarette fire in the couch cushions. It was 7:30 AM. Good news: nearly his bedtime.

⚡ The Lager-er's New Clothes ⚡

In 2005, the venerable Dutch beer maker Grolsch unveiled new packaging and introduced an amber ale to complement the Premium Lager they've been brewing for nearly four hundred years. "The redesign of the packaging is more attractive and contemporary, which will appeal to both our current Grolsch drinkers and attract new consumers," said Peter Gyimesi, a guy Grolsch pays handsomely to say such rose-colored things.

Like its predecessor, the new Grolsch bottle is green, though a slightly different shade, which Gyimesi assuredly describes as "eye-catching." I guess he's right, since I recently caught sight of a six-pack in my fridge next to a Ziploc bag full of some nasty-looking brown stuff I prayed was leftover meatloaf (the lesson here: never walk your dog while intoxicated). The new logo isn't all that different from the old one, although I guess you could say it's a bit more "todayish" than it was yesterday. (Take that, Gyimesi!)

Bottomfeeder is my landlord's nephew and he lives on my sofa. Not just sleeps there, *lives* there. Rent-free. Like a homeless guy on a park bench, except with access to my fridge and beer and cable TV. Why? Well, due to a complex legal settlement—struck shortly after a cooking experiment gone wrong resulted in a large, ridiculously destructive grease fire in my building—well, I can't get into exactly *why* he lives on my sofa. I *can* tell you that Bottomfeeder is unemployed, out of shape, quite possibly in need of some sort of intervention, *and* spends nearly all of his nonsupine time figuring out creative ways to grow facial hair.

He has several equally degenerate friends, and collectively they refer to themselves as the UBC: the Unacceptable Behavior Club.

They'll start up in a bar: "Hey, are YOU-BEE-SEE?" I always wonder if they know that it could be taken as, "Are you Before Christ?" But crossing them in bars is a good way to get a quick head-butting lesson, so I keep my comments to myself.* None of them have jobs, either. They're also, perhaps because of the head-butting, very loud talkers. And they're always at my apartment, like somebody dropped off an obstreperous group of agitated Doberman pinschers.

"Am I the only guy in the world who misses the bottom part of the screen?" the Bottomfeeder is shouting as I labor to complete this chapter.

"What the hell are you talking about, man?"

"The bottom of the screen. THE BOTTOM OF THE FUCKING TV SCREEN!" he shouts, skittering through the channels for emphasis. "CNN, MSNBC, ESPN—they all got messages and numbers and reports and stuff constantly streaming across the bottom of the screen, blocking the view. Who cares about information? Most of it don't mean nuthin'! The newsbabe has a great rack and I'm getting stock quotes?! The best stuff on TV is actually happening at the bottom of the screen! AND WE'RE ALL MISSING IT!!!"

See what I'm up against? The only reason I've not yet defenestrated Bottomfeeder is that there exists the potential to make a lot of money off his life. You see, despite his fantastic array of shortcomings, I have

---

* Nightlife Tip #107: Head-butting is grounds for ejection in most reputable establishments. So is administering an Atomic Wedgie, the ins and outs of which will be examined in detail in my next book, *Instant Asshole . . . Just Add Alcohol.*

no doubt that Bottomfeeder will someday be famous—perhaps even before this book is finished.* I know a few famous people, and they're very much like him. Perhaps his fame will come as a new kind of street-wise philosopher, or a circus act,† or as the host of one of those cable shows aimed at misogynistic, beer-swilling louts—sort of *Blue Collar TV* meets *The Gong Show*. We'll call it *Who Wants To Marry Exotic Facial Hair?* Hell, with any luck at all he could be the Gen-X Bukowski. They say the best way to write a great novel is to live a great novel, so maybe Bottomfeeder's on the way to creating a nice psycho-thriller.

Failing all that, it's still fairly likely that Bottomfeeder will enter the public consciousness en masse in a "News of the Weird"/*Weekly World News* cover story sort of way. And when that happens, I'll be ready, with family photos and signed release forms and free-clinic admission records ... because I've got the film, TV, and newsprint rights to his life. That's right—only cost me five hundred dollars, too. Due to a burst of insane optimism triggered by a dream involving the Dallas Cowboys cheerleaders, Bottomfeeder made some poor gambling decisions, then desperately needed to pay off an irate bookie. And I needed . . . well, *something*. He refused to move out in exchange for the dough, so we settled on a more creative, if somewhat long-term, option.

I bought his story.

We whipped up a common-law contract modeled after that warning they give during Major League Baseball games, so I have rights to "descriptions, photos, and accounts" of his life. I immediately

---

* This is what's known as "foreshadowing."

† He can fart the theme songs to several popular TV shows.

mailed the originals to a trusted family member who agreed to keep the document tucked under his bar.

And now I wait, like a literary vulture. Even my friends think it's a bit strange, but someday this sort of thing is bound to become common. Just watch: in five years the producers of shows like *Before They Were Rock Stars* will be running around the world signing buy-it-forward deals with every twelve-year-old with a guitar and inferior playground skills. And MTV will own the first-time serial rights to one in three inner-city kindergarten students. Or not. I'm not saying this is a sure thing. But, come to think of it, I'm cashing in already—because Bottomfeeder is already book fodder, and there's nothing he can do about it, even on the off chance that somebody reads this to him.

＋♀♍♀＋

The other night on the evening news, the babe with the great rack led with a piece on rising consumer confidence, and hot damn if I wasn't surprised they had the manpower to devote to that juicy scoop, given the LIVE TEAM COVERAGE of a fuckin' fluffy white flurry they're calling a snowstorm! Shopping and inclement weather are big news, folks . . . war, genocide, natural disasters, and criminal abuse of power at the highest levels of government are just filler until Sports comes on. Bah! It's enough to drive someone to drink, I tell ya—and in this case, I was driven yet again to Jameson Irish Whiskey.

The Irish are no strangers to misery—witness the Great Potato Famine and Sinead O'Connor's last three albums, for instance—but they sure have developed an effective method of coping with it. John

Jameson began producing his signature whiskey in Dublin way back in 1780, and for the past 227 years his people have been drowning their considerable sorrows in its toasted woody goodness. But in recent years, Jameson has become quite fashionable worldwide at the trendy watering holes of the breezy beau monde, where it's not uncommon to see happy hipsters shooting it straight or enjoying it in a gimlet or sour. In places that cater to a more proletarian clientele, you'll often find Jameson being used as one of the three ingredients in that most leg-wobbling of grog-shop concoctions, the **Car Bomb.**

⚡ Bombs away! ⚡

As many of the more intrepid pub crawlers out there are no doubt aware, the increasingly popular Car Bomb is a pretty simple conceit: combine an ounce each of Baileys Original Irish Cream and Jameson in a shot glass, drop the shot into half a pint of Guinness, and chug it down. Gathering solid information about the origin of the drink, on the other hand, proved to be quite a challenge. None of the usually reliable mixologists I contacted had any idea where the Car Bomb originated, but a few were quite sure I needed to settle some rather large bar tabs. I put in a call to a representative from Diageo (parent company of Guinness and Baileys) who wouldn't fess up, claiming only that the Car Bomb is an affront to the company's high-minded advisory to "drink responsibly." Yeah, whatever!

A cry for help sent out to members of my Imbiber column's "Preferred Readers Club" didn't shed much light on the history of the Car Bomb, either, but several replies spoke volumes about the drink's potency. "The ingredients in a Car Bomb are best compared to men and relationships," wrote Leigh Monk of Philadelphia. "Separate, they're great, but together they make me want to puke."

From Brian McCole, also from Philly: "I'm a happy Irish bartender at an Irish pub. I know I'm serving someone of questionable drinking age when a fresh face comes up to the bar and asks, 'Uh, sir, can I have three Irish Car Bombs?' At which point I immediately become a stern German bartender and demand, 'Your papers, please!'"

The final word on the matter came from Alli Joseph in Manhattan: "Anyone smart enough to know anything about something as obscure as the history of the Car Bomb is smart enough to avoid drinking them." Put THAT in your Guinness and chug it!

Unlike Scotch whisky, which is made with malt dried over an open peat fire, the barley used in Jameson is dried in a closed kiln, thus omitting the smoky flavor. The result is a spirit that is smooth, sweet, and spicy, retaining the crispness from the pot-still distillation. There are several varieties of Jameson to choose from, and shot lovers are advised to stick with the classic. Those in the mood for sipping can go with the charming twelve-year-old, or really step out and enjoy the Master Selection, aged eighteen to twenty-three years in Spanish sherry casks before finishing in bourbon barrels. However you take it, one thing's for sure: when it comes to Irish whiskey—to borrow a line* from Sinead's last decent record—nothing compares to Jameson.

America's most celebrated whiskey, of course, is bourbon, and the best-selling brand worldwide is Jim Beam. Ten years ago, while working at a newspaper in Phoenix, I had the pleasure of spending a few hours in the company of Beam's grandson, Booker Noe, who passed away in February 2004. When I met Booker, he was nearly seventy years old and carried his considerable weight around with the assistance of a wooden cane, but in all the ways that mattered he was still the same bourbon-swilling Kentucky boy who began learning the family business back in 1950.

"Our first label was called Old Tub, established in 1882," Booker told me. "My grandfather started that label. That first label had a picture of a black man mashing the bourbon in a tub, so they called it Old Tub."

He continued, "A lot of the bourbons are named 'old' something.

---

* . . . which she borrowed from Prince

Old Grand Dad. Old Crow. Old Tub. Old Bardstown." I wondered aloud why that was, and without missing a beat Booker said: "Because they're old."

In 1964 Congress declared bourbon a "distinctive product of the United States." Today, 98 percent of all the bourbon in the world is produced within a sixty-mile radius of Bardstown, Kentucky, the home of Jim Beam. The first bourbon labeled Jim Beam appeared after Prohibition.* Beam-made bourbon, however, dates back to 1795, when Jacob Beam sold his first barrel of whiskey. The barrel, it must be noted, is the key to good bourbon. By law, whiskey cannot be labeled bourbon unless it has been aged for a minimum of two years in new white-oak barrels that can be used only once. These barrels define the whiskey, giving it its color and adding considerable complexity to the raw spirit in much the way barrel-aging impacts the character of wine.

Booker told me that the difference between a wine hangover and a bourbon hangover† is that the histamines in wine make mornings after vino much, much worse. "Ohhh, yes," he said. "I've had these terrible, terrible headaches on that wine when I get too much of it. My wife says it's the histamines, so you got to take those antihistamines."

He spoke of a night when he and the late Carl Beam were taste-testing a batch of two-year-old bourbon that wasn't quite right. "We

---

* From 1920 to 1933, the Eighteenth Amendment made it illegal to manufacture, buy, sell, or transport liquor in the United States. It was thus a really shitty time to be a booze writer.

† The phrase "the hair of the dog that bit you" is widely believed to stem from an ancient Scottish superstition that called for treating dog-bite wounds with actual hair from the offending mutts to stave off infection.

were sitting up in Carl's office in this old beat-up wooden distillery," Booker reminisced, "and we drank up all the whiskey that we had there. We were feeling pretty good then, so I says I got to go. I better go on in. But Carl goes over to this cabinet of his and pulls out a half pint, and we finished that off—one for the road, you know, which you can't do no more, by the way." When Carl called Booker the next day to see how he was doing, Booker groaned, "To tell you the damn truth, I got the bust-head." The bust-head, he explained, is a hangover of such magnitude your head feels as if it might bust right open. I suspect that's a fairly accurate description of the way many bourbon lovers felt the day ole Booker Noe called it a life and headed up to the Great Whiskey Bar in the Sky.

As I finished that last sentence, Bottomfeeder, who has been lying on the sofa with his hand down his pants,* cranked up the television volume—his passive-aggressive way of letting me know the click-clack of the keyboard is bothering him. There was a report on CNN about researchers in Oregon who have concluded that gay sheep that mate only with other rams have different brain structures from "straight" sheep. Upon hearing this news I heaved a sigh of relief and thought, *Well, that clears that up.* Now, at long last, I can get back to monitoring the contentious battle between pro-life and pro-choice chickens.

"We are not trying to explain human sexuality by this study," said Charles Roselli, a professor of physiology and pharmacology who

---

* The reason men put their hands down their pants while they're watching TV isn't that we're itchy, it's so that the penis and the hand can spend a little, you know, quality nonsex time together.

supervised the gay-sheep analysis. This, of course, begs the obvious question: what the hell *were* they trying to explain? Perhaps they were hoping to eradicate antihomosexual sentiment in the sheep community. Lord knows, rams who are, shall we say, "light in the hooves" have suffered long enough. Well, rise up, all you effeminate, four-legged, woolly creatures, and say it loud, say it proud: "We're here, we're queer . . . and we're ready to be sheared!"

I must say that this study has raised a number of "counting sheep" issues that, quite frankly, I'm not sure I'm prepared to deal with. Really, if I count gay sheep at night, does that make *me* gay, or just curious? Aw, hell, I guess I'll count aborted chickens instead. And next up for Oregon researchers: studying the effects of long-term exposure to marijuana in sea lions.

·♀ ♀ ♀·

Now it's time once again to roll back the clock. . . .

Prior to becoming a world-renowned wine and spirits scribe, I landed a temporary gig writing booze-soaked humor columns for the AOL/Time Warner conglomerate, and I regret to admit that it didn't prove the choicest job in the world. Shortly after I accepted the position, the editor over at Warner Bros. called to let me know that despite her best efforts, and despite the REAL LOVE & AFFECTION everyone over there had for me, she'd been unable to finagle any actual *cash* from the WB Accounting Department, meaning that for the foreseeable future I would be paid in unwatchable DVDs and stuffed Looney Tunes dolls.

That's a real pisser, I thought, as I sat stroking my brand-new, nearly life-sized Tweety Bird at my local watering hole, O'Brien's Irish Pub. "I'M OFFICIALLY FREAKED OUT!!!!" I told Wes the Bartender. "I have no money, no high-paying assignments in the pipeline . . . and my only viable assets are half a bottle of whisky that somebody gave me and seventeen copies of *Summer Catch*." Thank goodness Wes is a Freddie Prinze Jr. fan, or I couldn't even cover the nut for my booze at O'Brien's.

I should "set the scene," as they say: it was 9:30 AM on a sunny Tuesday and I was twelve steps into what may have been the most unhealthy breakfast eaten by a human since Hannibal Lecter interned at the L.A. Coroner's Office. My Cranialmobile was running way too hot and hurtling head-on toward a BAD PLACE at the end of a LOST HIGHWAY. And I remind you . . . it was 9:30 AM.

"Christ, man, I can't even afford a decent meal," I cried, knocking back yet another stiff shot of Johnnie Walker Blue.*

"Well," Wes corrected me in a voice reserved for calming a first grader who has somehow found the family handgun, "you can't buy any breakfast you've been familiar with *up until this time*." Wes very carefully

---

* Easily the world's most luxurious blended whisky, each individually numbered bottle of JW Blue retails for approximately $210 (with a limited-edition cask-strength version also available for, ahem, $3,500 per bottle), and with good reason: as any serious Scotch drinker or pro palate will attest, Blue is a masterpiece of malt mixology. The closely guarded secret recipe includes some of the rarest whiskies in the world—including at least one, and perhaps several, aged more than half a century. The finished product is huskier than Kathleen Turner's voice, with the voluptuous body to match (Turner circa 1985, that is). Each sip delivers a deluge of flavors dominated by sweet spice and honey, complemented by not-so-subtle hints of tobacco and toffee. The smoky finish lingers like something that just doesn't want to go away, and is far more impressive than, say, random celebrity references and analogies.

topped off my shot glass before continuing. "See, down on 'The Nickel' (as they call Fifth Avenue, aka skid row, in L.A.) you can get a hot coffee for fifty cents . . . and the line outside the mission is a great place to meet fellow writers who have been at it longer than you. And you could trade some of that hippie whisky you've got for somebody's place in line . . . or even dole out swigs from the bottle for a dollar each."

For reasons I cannot comprehend, Wes's idea struck me as somewhat palatable, and that—as you can well imagine—disturbed me to no end. Then just when I thought my life's stock price couldn't fall any lower, Wes hit me between the eyes with this zinger: "Have you tried borrowing money from your mother?"

I'm a grown man, for chrissakes! I'd sooner smash my nuts with a hammer.

"Or you could get a part-time job waiting tables," he added.

I'd sooner hand my mother a hammer, and have *her* smash my nuts. Don't get me wrong: waiting tables is an honorable profession practiced by some of the finest people on the planet . . . it's just that, well, I don't have the PEOPLE SKILLS the job demands. And the only place I'm comfortable uttering the words, "Would you like that well done, miss?" is in my bedroom, preferably when speaking to a supermodel—one with an unusual name, like Uniti or Gioa. Or both.

"Boy, that Freddie Prinze Jr. is a fine actor," Wes suddenly gushed, ogling the DVD cover and letting his eyes roam to my freshly poured hootch. "Can you get me some more of his movies?"

"What? Um, yeah, I might be able to get my hands on a bootleg copy of *Wing Commander*. . . . Say, Wes, did you ever have to resort to desperate measures to get by when you were down on your luck?"

A broad smile crept across Wes's face as he rolled back to the lean years of his youth. Either that, or he was still thinking about the amazing screen presence of Freddie Prinze Jr.

"When we lived in Ventura just after college," he waxed, "our thing was to go buy a dollar Bud at happy hour and then eat at the buffet for, like, an hour."

It was then that I began wondering why in the hell O'Brien's didn't have dollar Buds or a buffet I could plunder—hell, I'd be satisfied with some pretzel mix just like the old days at Cooper Street in Aspen. And it struck me that Wes always spoke of a "we" in his anecdotes—who the hell were these people? And how did *they* escape all this poverty? Were they, perhaps, the source of all this semicredible "on The Nickel" knowledge?

"No kidding," Wes continued. "In some places they got so they wouldn't serve us. Finally I slimed my way into writing a feature story on the 'happy-hour buffet wars' for the *Ventura County Star*—it was the *Star-Free Press* in those days—and made many friends. What you need is a good restaurant review column on that new Web site. That ought to help matters."

I made a mental note to run the restaurant-review idea by my editor at Warner Bros. Then I worked out a contingency plan, that being to stock up on instant oatmeal. I figured that even if they cut off the electric and gas, in a large complex such as mine they couldn't cut off the hot water to only one apartment very easily. There are also hot-water taps at the coffee stations of most 7-11 stores these days, but you have to bring your own cup or they'll charge you an "inventory" fee. Or, I reasoned, I could find a sponsor for the Warner Bros. column—perhaps the good people at Johnnie Walker, makers of fine whiskies of the Black and Red and Blue varieties.*I was warming to the idea: tie in a little e-commerce with those red-hot *Summer Catch* discs on eBay . . .

Instead, I decided to participate in that great Hollywood ritual: the Day Job.

. ♕ ♔ ♕ .

Keri, the gal at the employment agency, seemed enthusiastic enough—at first. By the end of my Career Connection Meeting, however, she had trouble concealing her serious misgivings about me and/or my employability. Who could blame her? With the possible exception of being able to string together a few not-quite-witty sentences now and then, I had few viable skills that fit into the modern workplace, which to this day remains starkly devoid of high-paying jobs for experts in sports trivia and shadow puppeteering. As for aptitudes or interests, it was probably a mistake to supply the restraining order, even though it answered those application questions better than I ever could. So, in other words, I was—and, some would argue, continue to be—woefully short on skills for which sober people in their right minds might be willing to pay me actual currency.

---

* I reiterate, people, that this is a serious blend that is not to be trifled with, and it is highly recommended that even seasoned whisky drinkers cut JW Blue with a wee bit of ice water. If you desire to effect a Rat Pack mystique or are simply the sort who insists on tossing every spirit into a cocktail, your best bet is a Manhattan made with two parts Johnnie Blue and one part dry vermouth. And while it's not my concoction of choice, I've got a drinking buddy with impeccable taste who swears by Rob Roys made with Blue, sweet vermouth, and a dash of Angostura bitters.

"How would you characterize your phone skills?" Keri asked, tapping a pencil on her handset for emphasis.

"I wouldn't," I replied, smart enough to know she wouldn't ask a phone-sex question that early in the process. "At least not in the course of any conversation I'm used to having."

"C'mon," she prodded, "how good are you on the phone?"

"Um, well, I've never had any complaints," I demurred. "Generally, the phone rings, I answer it, and when the conversation is over, I hang up . . . pretty standard."

"How many lines do you think you could handle at once?" she asked.

Sounded like a trick question. My roommate, the Bottomfeeder, has often warned me that it's "common street knowledge" that employment agents are trained in FBI interrogation techniques. They are taught to carefully poke and prod in the hopes of exposing any gross character deficiencies before they send you off to work at some large corporation with a team of highly paid attorneys.

"Geez, I dunno, Keri. I've never really . . . I never . . . I don't know."

"C'mon, how many lines could you handle? Take a guess."

I was getting jittery. I started to sweat. Keri kept tapping the phone with the pencil, and her co-workers began eyeing me suspiciously. I had suspected from the beginning that the Career Connection Meeting was a bad idea, and now my suspicions were coming home to roost. Damn unemployment! And damn mixed metaphors! "HOW MANY LINES COULD YOU HANDLE?" Keri demanded. At least I *think* she demanded to know. My mind plays tricks when the heat is on. And it doesn't help that in such situations I often turn to inappropriate humor.

"It depends on how many lines I did before I got to work," I blurted.

This, of course, was not the correct answer. Yet it was also not a "get the hell out before I call the police"–type answer, either, because that era's Employee Glut hadn't yet hit the L.A. temporary-office-employment demographic. It turns out Keri was hard up for flunkies, and I had a capital "F" stamped on my forehead.

"I just got something that might be perfect for you," she said, flipping through a stack of job listings.

"Oh, yeah?"

"A Film Buff Convention needs a Corey Haim impersonator."

"A Corey Haim impersonator? But . . . but I don't look anything like Corey Haim!"

"Sure you do: the puppy-dog eyes; the curly brown hair. Um, a mouth. Ears. You're perfect for the job."

"Well, I always have been a fan of *License To Drive*," I found myself saying. Funny how desperation can make us say and do things we'd never consider under normal circumstances. I didn't realize until that moment how much "seeking work" could resemble "picking up dates" or "impressing former high school buddies." Calls were quickly placed to the right important people, but unfortunately it seemed that Corey Haim was already being impersonated by a former child actor who had just gotten bumped from a gig parking cars in Malibu. I know what you're thinking, but the car-parking company required a full background check, and who needs that?

"How about audience member?" Keri asked.

"Come again?"

"Would you be interested in being an audience member?" she said with a smile.

That part of my brain in charge of Smart Remarks went into overdrive. A decade of spiritual doubt left my body, because only a universe in the full and constant control of a Divine Being would force a test of my words. What would it be? A witty retort about mingling with the mutants on *The Price Is Right*? A but-gusting joke about a night in the Peanut Gallery with the Jerry Springer faithful?

"So," I said, "they actually *pay* audience members?"

"Right," she replied. "Not much: six dollars an hour, plus a snack."

At that, my self-control levee broke.

"Six bucks? For six bucks I wouldn't watch the show at home in my underwear drinking cold beer, let alone show up at a studio."

"But I haven't told you what the show is. . . ."

"Yes, you have," I interrupted as I got up out of the chair, wondering if the people moving slowly in the back were about to call the cops. Maybe my voice had suddenly risen to what some would think inappropriate levels. "You've told me it's a show where they pay people to sit in the audience, and that's plenty."

It felt better on the street in the warm embrace of another unemployed L.A. afternoon. It had been worth the try, and the Abercrombie & Fitch shirt could be worn again despite its small underarm stains. Keri would never call, but so what? Believe it or not,* there remained yet another option: perhaps it was time to try my hand at becoming a screenwriter.

---

* The best bet is not to believe it.

+ ♉ 🏆 ♉ +

The first time I phoned, after one of those just-too-long pauses, he "wasn't in." So I left a brief, casual-yet-firm message on Mr. Fong's voice mail. Eight frustrating days and four unreturned calls later, I called again and finally got someone on the line who identified herself as Mr. Fong's assistant.

"He's not available right now," she hissed, her voice dripping with contempt. "You'll have to leave your number."

"I've left my number too many damn times already," I counter-hissed, my patience wearing thinner than Kate Moss on a three-month protein diet.

"I'm sorry, who did you say you were with?"

"With? I'm not *with* anyone, and what difference does it . . . look, could you please just explain to me WHY Mr. Fong is unfailingly unavailable?"

"Mr. Fong is in a meeting."

Sure, L.A. has its challenges. Homicidal traffic. Corrupt cops. High rent and earthquakes. Hordes of people who dress better than you. It all goes with the town. But nobody should have to take this kind of abuse.

"Mr. Fong," I told his assistant, "is *always* in a meeting. Everyone in this damn town is *always* in a meeting. Tell me—because you seem to be very astute—is anybody in Los Angeles capable of . . . of . . . of doing *anything* without having a meeting about it first?"

"Sure," she sneered. Click.

Hey, did I mention that Mr. Fong was my dry cleaner? Check

that: Mr. Fong was my *Hollywood* dry cleaner. That does not, of course, necessarily mean that he was located in Hollywood, any more than I live "in" L.A. (Santa Monica is its own city, now isn't it?) It's a case of attitude outranking geography. But being a Hollywood dry cleaner meant that Mr. Fong took meetings all day long. I'm sure these included important concept-development sessions with the screen-writer who drove the delivery truck, the actress who worked the steam press, and the producer who parked cars at the restaurant across the street—all of whom, incidentally, would likely have ignored my calls as well, had the opportunity presented itself. This pervasive snubbish-ness stems from the commonly held notion that, at any given moment, one's standing in the Hollywood community can be meas-ured in direct proportion to who you can afford not to call back. It's a brutal food chain—and the only possible reason I often go weeks without calling my mother.

"The callback is how you let people know what kind of leverage you've got in this town," explained my friend and quasi-career coun-selor Wendy, who had recently been elevated to the rank of junior executive at a cable network. Wendy celebrated her promotion by waiting nearly three days before returning a call to former *Two Close for Comfort* star Jim J. Bullock. She likened my stints as a rather suc-cessful newspaper columnist in Aspen and Phoenix to being a big fish in a little pond.

"Yeah, yeah, yeah. And now that I'm in L.A., I'm just a little fish in a big pond, right?" I grumbled, making a mental note to remove the "fish" line from the dialogue in my first screenplay, *Fun Things to Do with Mud.*

She shook her head.

"No? Well, what am I then?"

"Pond scum. Don't take it personally."

"*Pond scum?*"

"Yes," she said in a voice reserved for telling twelve-year-olds they hadn't made the team. "But we're going to change all that. People are going to start calling you back soon enough. Hell, someday they'll even call without you having to call them first."

To that heady end, Wendy took a treatment I had written and passed it on to an agent friend of hers—a real hotshot who had recently started his own agency after several years of grooming at UTA or CAA or ADD or someplace like that. She told me he was going to call me, and that his name was Fisher.

"What's his first name?" I asked. "Or should I just call him Mr. Fisher?"

"No, silly. Fisher *is* his first name."

I tried, unsuccessfully, to suppress a giggle.

"What's the matter? Haven't you ever met a guy named Fisher?"

"I grew up in a tough neighborhood in Philly," I told Wendy. "Abandoned crack babies have a better survival rate than boys named Fisher. With a name like that, he would have been snowballed to death in preschool."

"You best be nice to Fisher," Wendy advised. "He's big-time. He can really help your career."

There seemed no reason to ask the obvious question: if Fisher was so big-time, what the hell was he doing calling me? Perhaps his doctor told him he wasn't getting enough pond scum in his diet. It didn't matter. The only thing that did matter was that I had finally arrived in Hollywood. Somebody would be calling *me*. And soon. When the call finally came, you can bet I was doubly impressed that it came from Fisher's secretary, who then patched me through to Fisher's cell phone. Apparently, there is a subcategory in this Hollywood Phone Call food chain that has to do with the actual pushing of the buttons and "where" you take the call. For instance, anyone talking "first-look" deals through a mouthful of McNuggets is likely slipping down the ladder. If, on the other hand, you get someone on the line who asks you to hold on while he adjusts the palm-frond-waving rate of the Nubian boys in his suite at the Peninsula, well, you might be getting somewhere.

"So a couple of thoughts on your movie idea," said Fisher, the sound of rush-hour traffic in the background. "First off, my friend, you gotta lose the strip club . . . why not a nice restaurant instead?"

"Well," I replied, "I set it in the strip club because . . ."

"JESUS CHRIST, YOU FUCKING MORON!"

"Excuse me?"

"Sorry. Some asshole just cut me off on Melrose," Fisher said. "Look, bottom line, I think we've got something here. Maybe the restaurant won't work. But you've got 'mud' in the title; maybe we can set it in a dry cleaners."

"A dry cleaners?"

"Yeah, my development partner would love it. Great guy named Fong, runs a little joint on the Westside. His delivery guy is a great touch-up script doctor and . . ."

A better man would have hung up. Instead I told Fisher that it sure was a small town and I was tight with Fong's secretary, and in fact thought she was a bit *hung up* on me. I made a mental note to add that "hung up" line to the *Mud* script and listened to him until he lost signal midsentence near the 405. When he called back, I let it ring five times before picking it up. Practicing.

· ♈ ♈ ♈ ·

"Practicing what?" Bottomfeeder asked, peering over my shoulder and causing me to fall out of step on my march down memory lane.

"Dammit, man," I howled, angrily swiveling around in my chair. "What did I tell you about doing that?"

"What? Why? Is this shit expensive?" he asked, referring to the pricey bottle of Scotch from which he'd just taken a large swig.

"No! I mean, *yes*, it *is* expensive. Really expensive. Particularly for someone like you who doesn't have a goddamn job!" The remark seemed to sting him, at least momentarily, which would explain the

⚡ A Compendium of the Most Popular of the Brown Spirits ⚡

To "E" or Not to "E"

Scotland, Canada, and Japan produce "whisky"; everyplace else spells it "whiskey." Nobody really knows the definitive reasoning behind the vowel disparity, but there's no doubt it has been a source of great debate over the years in many a heated game of Scrabble.

Jack and Jim

No, it's not the name of a gay sitcom on Bravo—I'm referring to Jack Daniels and Jim Beam, which many people, including a lot of bartenders, erroneously believe to be two different

continued on next page >>

abashed look on his face as he swallowed even more of the whisky. "But I'm talking about reading over my shoulder. Like I've told you a million times already—it messes me up, dammit!"

"*O-kay*, but do you think anybody is actually going to *care* about this dude Fang? He's not even *real*, is he?" Bottomfeeder said.

"It's *Fong*, and I guess we won't know until the book comes out, will we?" I shot back. "Which isn't ever going to happen if you don't learn to respect my boundaries, man. I can't work like this!"

"You know, you're right, brutha," he said, filling an empty Big Gulp with copious amounts of my **whisky**. "I do remember promising not to drink directly from the bottle anymore, and I'm sorry." Then he swilled another big gulp from the Big Gulp. "Damn! This is some *serious shit*, right? Expensive?"

"You could say that, yeah," I replied. Scapa's 1980 vintage single malt is virtually impossible to find for less than three hundred dollars. They only released two thousand hand-numbered bottles back in '05 after twenty-five years of aging in traditional oak casks, and to my

---

brands of the same whiskey. JD is a Tennessee whiskey. Beam is bourbon. Both are concocted from a mash that is at least 51 percent corn, but in Tennessee they filter the spirit through a special maple charcoal.

Characteristics
Scotch is smoky, bourbon oaky, and Irish whiskey O'kay.

Schools of Thought
The latest trend is to drink whiskey neat—it's more "authentic." But if you do, a couple drops of chilled branch water can really open up the taste. Kick it old school with a "Tall Water," which is a tall glass of ice water with a single shot of whiskey stirred in.

great dismay that limited supply was diminishing before my eyes. Scapa tastes like the best piece of ass you've ever had, if you're strange or adventurous enough to have had whisky-soaked ass.*

Bottomfeeder announced that he was going bowling and took the Scapa with him. He wasn't out the door five seconds when I Googled the words "complete lunatic" and "help please" and came across a story about an American Airlines pilot who had decided to extol the virtues of Christianity and refer to all non-Christians as "crazy" during a 2004 flight from Los Angeles to New York. It didn't strike me as a big deal at first. After all, what's the worst thing that could happen when a religious fundamentalist sits at the controls of a large aircraft? But as more and more details were made available about the incident, it became clear to me that a Great Evil was at work on American Flight 34 that day. First off, the pilot, Rodger Findiesen, admitted he'd encouraged Christian passengers to use their time in the air to talk to the infidels . . . er, the *non-Christian* travelers, about their faith. Second, the in-flight movie was *My Boss's Daughter*.

I ask you, folks, what kind of God would condemn innocent people to spend five hours in a pressurized tube with a bunch of babbling Bible thumpers *and* Ashton Kutcher? Certainly not the God my

---

* On the lighter and sweeter side is a delightful sixteen-year-old single malt from Balblair, Scotland's second-oldest distillery. This award-winning label ($49.99) is eminently drinkable, and makes an excellent gateway to huskier whiskies such as Lagavulin. In short, Balblair kicks butt. The Famous Grouse offers a blended whisky ($34.99) comprised of twelve-year-old single malts from the likes of Highland Park and the Macallan, which—not so coincidentally—fall under the same ownership umbrella. The Grouse is the mellowest and most citrusy of the bunch—the kind of whisky you drink on the rocks when you just wanna chill out.

parents forced me to believe in! Factor in the five-dollar charge for headphones, and it's pretty obvious that Satan was up to his old tricks again and that those passengers were literally on the Flight from Hell.*

Findiesen, it turned out, was an Evangelical Christian who'd recently returned from doing mission work in Costa Rica. While I don't profess to be completely up to speed on the tenets of Evangelical Christianity, I do know that the breed seems awfully fond of quoting Scripture at ball games and that they tolerate sinners in much the same way the Chinese government recognizes civil liberties. I'm not saying that Findiesen was a bona fide bag of mixed nuts, but we do have to consider what might have transpired if, after he'd asked the Christians to raise their hands thirty minutes into the flight, he hadn't been satisfied with the head count. Let's not forget the Muslim pilot who praised Allah over the intercom on an Egyptian plane a few years back just before rerouting the jet to a permanent layover at the bottom of the ocean. Findiesen didn't crash Flight 34, but that's not to say that kind of disaster couldn't occur in the future. According to "Rapture Ready," a Web site devoted to monitoring the imminent return of

---

* This got me thinking about a drink I concocted to numb my senses on a flight to Borneo in which I was sandwiched between a hyperactive personal-injury lawyer and a deodorant-deficient colporteur. The Devil in the Sky is a fiery fix-ya-up that's sure to singe any traveler's frazzled nerve endings. You'll need airplane bottles of Absolut Peppar and Everclear 190, Tabasco sauce, and salt (ingredients available on most Air Lush connections). Put six drops of Tabasco in the bottom of a shot glass, add equal parts Peppar and Everclear, then top with salt. Discreetly set on fire with the lighter you smuggled on board, serve, and pray there are no air marshals on the plane.

Christ to Earth so he can reclaim his most devout followers, Christians like Findiesen are due to disappear into thin air any day now.

"There has never been a time in history when the return of the Lord has been so near," the site proclaims. "We need to hold the things of this world—money, homes, ambitions—with an open hand, ready to drop it all at the beckoning of our Lord."

What if the Lord were to beckon while Findiesen was flying another 747 over the Rockies? The heathens on board had better *pray* the copilot had been taking the Lord's name in vain or, better yet, fondling a stewardess in the Admiral's Lounge before takeoff. And will any professional sports franchises besides the Portland Trailblazers and the Cincinnati Bengals be able to field a team after the Rapture? Like me, your head's probably filled with all sorts of questions like these right now. Fortunately, "Rapture Ready" offers plenty of answers in a convenient FAQ.

The site clears up various mysteries: about whether angels are real ("Absolutely!"), the Antichrist is Jewish (yes, "because the Jews will not receive a Gentile as their promised Messiah"), and AIDS is a judgment from God (yes, if contracted while engaged in "sexual relations outside of marriage, homosexual activity, and drug use"; no for those "who have contracted HIV through no fault of their own"). Worried about those New Age Hippies from California who just moved in next door? You should be, Christian Soldier, because "New Agers focus much energy on world peace, environmental pursuits and disarmament . . . New Age thinking has subtly infiltrated every part of life in this country. Yoga, meditation, self-discovery, inner being . . . these are all terms that are closely associated with the New Age

movement. So, beware! The devil wants to deceive you and this movement is one of his very effective tools!"

I couldn't find anything in the FAQ about what to do should the
pilot of your cross-country flight begin speaking in tongues over the
intercom, or what can be done to stop all the fucking nutcases with
Web sites on the Internet, but I was thrilled to learn that masturba-
tion "would appear to be a common function of sexuality" and thus is
permissible, so long as I'm not thinking about my neighbor's wife
while I do it. Ha! My neighbor doesn't have a wife—he's gay! Then
again, if this gay-marriage thing sticks and he and his partner get
hitched and I happen to see the boys sunning out in the garden and .
. . first the sheep counting, and now this. Oh, Christ, I'm damned.

Being an in-demand member of the international drinking press,
I'm used to writing about liquor from inside pressurized metal tubes
thirty-five thousand feet up in the air. And while I've not experienced
anything quite so peculiarly frightening as the Findiesen flare-up, I've
had more than a few funky experiences aboard airplanes—for instance,
the time I wound up on a cross-country flight sitting next to an inquis-
itive and highly flatulent eight-year-old. Little Lance was on his way to
New York from Los Angeles to visit his grandmother. I was headed
there to hang out with movie stars and get drunk at the Tribeca Film
Festival.* One time after he passed wind, Lance politely excused

---

* The list of scheduled attendees—stamped with a big fat "A"—included Tom Cruise, John Tra-
volta, Robert DeNiro, James Gandolfini, Naomi Watts, Matt Dillon, Kurt Russell, Trudy Styler,
John Malkovich, Brendan Fraser, Peter Krause, Jeff Goldblum, Jeff Garlin, and Sarah Silverman,
to name a few (fourteen, actually).

himself and began giggling uncontrollably. Moments later and for no apparent reason, he reached up, pushed the flight-attendant call button, and turned off my air vent while explaining that it was the longest flight he'd ever been on by himself. It started to feel that way for me, too.

"What's that you're drinking?" he asked, pointing to a half-empty bottle of the Glenrothes Select Reserve on my tray table.

"It's called whisky," I said. "Do you know what that is?"

He shook his head no, and then in one prodigious slurp polished off an entire juice box.

"Why do you need such a big bottle?" he asked.

"I'm a big guy," I told him.

"It smells."

"Yeah, well, so do you."

This set Lance to giggling again. I was pretty happy, too, actually, because the Glenrothes Select Reserve is a real treat. It's a Speyside whisky, and if you don't know what that means, well, fire up Google cuz you've got a lot of catching up to do. Until 2006, The Glenrothes produced only vintage single malts that cost beaucoup bucks. Select Reserve is a blend of casks from an assortment of vintages and is as affordable ($45 per 750 ml bottle) as it is tasty. Fruity and smooth, Select Reserve is certainly one of the mildest, easiest-drinking whiskies I've sampled in some time.

As for little Lance, he spent most of the rest of the flight sleeping—that is, until just before landing, when I caught whiff of something and spied him curled up on his seat with a guilty look on his face. An attractive woman seated across the aisle crinkled her nose and shot me a look of disgust. Thanks a LOT, kid!

Step 4

The Tequila Sunrise Also Rises
(Provided You Drink Too Many)

I was a good half hour into *Alan Thicke's Pool Guy: The E! True Hollywood Story* when it dawned on me that the boundaries of celebrity have been stretched beyond what a sane person might consider reasonable limits. Of course, reason and sanity have no place in the twenty-first-century cult of personality, where fame can be achieved by virtually anyone who possesses nothing more than a willingness to embarrass themselves on television. That cruel fact reminded me that I needed to call my agent to check on a TV series project that—unbeknownst to my bosses at the newspaper—I'd been developing on the side.

"We're definitely getting some nibbles," Fisher chirped over a godawful racket that sounded like nothing so much as a sty full of piglets being set ablaze.

"Where are you, man?" I queried.

"On the set of a new music video for Vanessa Minnillo* and Nick Lachey. Don't they sound amazing?"

---

* This sort-of celebrity's name sort of rhymes with Thrilla Vanilla, a French vanilla liqueur for DeKuyper. I used to think real men didn't drink French vanilla liqueur, until I tried it with bourbon and cola on the rocks. It'll put hair on your chest . . . you can have it waxed off later.

"Are you representing them?"

"Well, sort of," Fisher fudged. "I'm shepherding a project Manny developed."

"Who's *Manny?*"

"Nick's personal trainer's assistant. The kid's got 'star' written all over him."

A good quip regarding the need for an eraser immediately came to mind, and I made a note to add it to the treatment for my latest sitcom idea, *Up the River, Down the River,* about an escaped convict who flees to South America and winds up living with a family of Yanomamö Indians along the banks of the Amazon. And yes, it *is* as funny as it sounds.

"The guys over at Fox like the convict element," Fisher said, "but they think you should take the guy out of the Amazon and instead make him a disgraced female Democratic vice-presidential candidate who winds up running a brothel full of wacky prostitutes in New Orleans. They're talking to Polly Holliday's people about the lead."

"A disgraced Democratic vice-presidential candidate? Polly Holliday? What the hell are you talking about?"

"Yeah, you know, Flo from *Alice*. Remember?" he enthused. "Kiss mah grits!"

"Kiss mah grits?"

"Oh, man, was that a great catchphrase or what?" he said. "Anyhoo, assuming you're cool with those minor alterations, the network might be interested in looking at a pilot provided you write it on spec and agree to change the name of the show."

"The name?"

"That's right, they want to call it *Polly's Pros*." Pretty catchy, eh?"

I stared at the television for a long while, saying nothing while Fisher repeatedly asked if I was still on the line. Finally, having at least partially digested the load of shit he'd just fed me, I uttered the first thought that came to mind:

"You know what I think, Fisher? I think I'd like to knit the world a giant sweater using the thread that comes with every purchase at Banana Republic."

"Uh-huh," he muttered uneasily, his usual reaction whenever I tossed these sorts of curveballs in his direction.

"I've got, literally, hundreds of those tiny spools of thread, which speaks volumes about my personal fashion sense," I continued. "Truth be told, I'm an Urban Outfitters–type personality, but those tight retro tees and hip-hugging low-riders simply do not flatter my ever-expanding love handles and man boobs."

Fisher drew a deep breath. "Right. So I'll go back to the network and let 'em know we're on board with *Polly's Pros?*"

"Alan Thicke's pool guy has a hot wife," I replied.

"Okay then, great," he bubbled. "I'm really feeling an Emmy nomination down the line for this one, Double-D. I've already got Manny working on a way-cool theme song."

"Fisher?"

"Yeah, buddy?"

"Kiss mah grits."

• ♀ ♀ ♀ •

Days later I completed a draft of a pilot script for the *Polly's Pros* sitcom, and boy, I gotta tell ya, it was beyond doubt the steamiest piece of dung I've ever penned. And those of you who've been paying attention these last few chapters know that that's really saying something. The network, of course, loved it.

Here's the skinny on the show: A disgraced former Democratic vice-presidential candidate, played by Polly Holliday, winds up running a brothel full of wacky prostitutes in New Orleans. In the first episode, Polly finds herself up to her neck in blue-balled customers and broke-ass hos after a strike at the Trojan condom factory threatens to shut down her operation. But then one of the working girls comes up with a plan to save the whorehouse that involves getting everyone so drunk that they don't care about using rubbers anymore.

Genius, I thought, as I typed "The End," given that I had zero interest in actually seeing *Polly's Pros* become a reality. I was certain that once the execs over at Fox had a look at the script's first two or three pages they'd scrap the whole damn project, then have me tossed off the lot. This would free me up to go elsewhere to pitch my original idea for *Up the River, Down the River*. Instead, the clowns at Fox bought the *Polly's Pros* pilot and immediately arranged a brainstorming meeting for me with an effeminate junior development exec named Barry. I brought Fisher along to run interference once things invariably got out of hand.

"LOVE the part about the girl who comes up with the idea to save Polly's Place," Barry gushed. "Who do you envision playing that role?"

"Nobody, to be honest," I said bitterly. "In fact, I can't believe that you guys even—"

"Even have to ask!" Fisher jumped in. "That part was made for Tracy Nelson."

"Tracy Nelson? From *Square Pegs?*" Barry asked. "She's a client of yours?"

"Well, used to be," Fisher replied. "She fired me when *The Father Dowling Mysteries* got cancelled. But we're talking again. I think she'd be perfect for this."*

"Isn't she old? Like, fortysomething?"

"She plays early twenties, though," Fisher fibbed.

I'd had enough already. "Tracy Nelson can't play a hooker on this show!" I shouted. "Who would pay to screw Tracy Nelson?"

"We don't ever want to refer to the girls as hookers," admonished Barry, who damn sure wouldn't screw Tracy Nelson . . . the Nelson twins, maybe, as in the late Ricky's† Johnny Winteresque middle-aged sons.

"But they *are* hookers," I shot back.

"Yes," he said, "but they're NETWORK TV hookers. They can't have sex or do drugs or behave in any way that is actually hooker-like. That would upset the sponsors."

---

* Father Dowling was played by Tom Bosley, best known for his role as Mr. Cunningham on *Happy Days*. However, I'm most fond of the work Bosley did in those Glad trash bag commercials.

† Onetime heartthrob Ricky Nelson died in a plane crash in Texas in 1985 while on his way to a New Year's Eve concert. In a related note, more champagne is consumed on New Year's Eve than on any other night of the year.

"It's the same thing with gays,"* Fisher chimed in as Barry nodded in agreement.

I continued to harp on the inanity of doing a show about hookers in which we'd never allude to the fact that they turn tricks for a living, but Barry would not be swayed. People would tune in because *Polly's Pros* would be a show about *real* people, not sex, he claimed. The fact that these *real* people just happen to work in a brothel is purely incidental. Oh yeah? Tell that to the johns.

"One last thing—the network has a problem with some of the language in the pilot," Barry said.

"The language? What language?"

"Squeeze my tits."

"That's her catchphrase," I explained. "Like 'kiss mah grits,' only with a little more oomph."

His face betrayed no emotion, but I could see at that moment that Barry hated me like a fashion model hates carbohydrates. "You can't say 'squeeze my tits' on network television," he hissed through a forced smile.

"*Really?*" I shot back in an intentionally annoying matter-of-fact manner. "I didn't think 'tits' were bad."

"Well, they *are* bad," sneered Barry, getting up from his seat to signal the meeting's end. "But we're sure you'll be able to come up with something else."

Figures he'd say that . . . about the tits, I mean.

---

* According to the best guess of a popular wine and spirits columnist, the most popular cocktail in the gay community is the Cosmopolitan, followed by the Blow Job.

"Maybe I can tweak it a little once I'm back from Mexico," I said.

This stopped Barry in his light loafers. "Mexico? Why? And for how long?"

"A few days," Fisher interjected.

"I'm thinking at least two weeks," I countered. "Possibly a month."

"Do you think that's really *responsible*, Dan?" Barry sniveled.

"I'm sure the people signing my checks at the newspaper would say it is," I shot back.

"Well, just remember what your main priority needs to be here," Barry advised.

"Oh, I'd *never* forget that."

＋ 𝖄 𝖄 𝖄 ＋

Remember that wonderful scene in *Caddyshack* in which Chevy Chase seduces a young woman with the aid of a few Tequila Slammers? Chevy snorts salt, swallows lime, tosses tequila. It's serious high comedy, and in more ways than one. You see, as anyone born prior to the 1980 release of *Caddyshack* probably suspected, there's no "right" answer for the which-one-first tequila-shot sequence. Turns out tequila isn't meant to be set up with salt, slammed, or chased with a giant wedge of lime.

A drink called the Bandera is one of the things travelers to Mexico eventually discover. Granted, it's not up there with the major cultural lessons like avoiding tap water or understanding that those young men in tattered Levi's toting automatic weapons on the street corners are there only to ensure your peace of mind, but it does add some spice to the consumption of Mexico's national adult beverage. Named for the Mexican flag, the Bandera consists of three ingredients, each served separately in tall shot glasses. First up, representing the flag's green stripe, is lime juice. If you can get them—and you usually can, in reputable establishments—go with Persian limes, which are sweeter and yellower than the American variety. In the middle glass goes the tequila. I recommend a good reposado such as Tradicional by Cuervo, although **Don Julio** Silver is quite nice as well. In the final glass goes a red shot of sangrita, which is essentially superspicy Bloody Mary mix. As for the proper drinking order, there isn't one. It's freestyle. Sip some tequila, then a little lime juice. Or go with tequila, sangrita, lime. Mix, match, have fun. You've graduated, friend. The finer things in life are yours for the drinking.

Granted, there's nothing particularly fancy about the place where I gathered the Bandera information—Nogales, a dusty Mexican shantytown-cum-city* along the Arizona border. In fact, it's what

⚔ A Time-Out for Tequila ⚔

Of all the momentous events of 1942, among them the premiere of *Casablanca* and the births of Cassius Clay, Paul McCartney, and Manolo Blahnik, perhaps nothing ranks as more historically consequential than the founding of a tequila distillery in Los Altos, Mexico, by a seventeen-year-old named Don Julio González . . . at least, that's the consensus among hardcore tequila drinkers, and really, does anyone else matter? Today, Don Julio is the luxury brand of choice for many a sophisticated tippler, but back in the '40s, when tequila was known as "mescal wine," it wasn't exactly the sort of spirit being served in the haunts of the haut monde. Young Señor González helped change that by producing tequila made only from prime sweet blue agave grown in a near-perfect microclimate around his hometown of Atotonilco el Alto.

continued on next page >>

* And unless you're interested in a sudden change in your employment status, I wouldn't recommend Googling "shantytown-cum-city" from any office computer that might be monitored.

travel professionals might refer to as a complete fucking shithole. Aesthetics aside, Nogales *is* of great interest to many American citizens in the Southwest, primarily because of the large number of shops there that provide easy access to cheap pharmaceuticals such as Viagra, Cialis, and Levitra.* They also sell plenty of heart medication down there, no doubt because all that chemically assisted sex takes its toll on old geezers' tickers. Since 1994, when the North American Free Trade Agreement (NAFTA) was enacted, American businesses—predominantly from the tech sector—have also been making a run for the border, shifting their manufacturing operations to maquiladoras.† Eighteen-year-old kids from Arizona go there on the weekends because they can legally drink. So do I, because I like getting bombed with teenagers-cum-young adults.° . . . You know, purely as a means of predicting future trends in the spirits industry.

I'm hoi polloi to the core, so I spent the bulk of my time in Mexico talking to "real" Mexicans in hopes of discovering the "real"

A few years ago, in commemoration of Don Julio's sixtieth anniversary of making tequila, the company introduced Tequila Don Julio 1942 ($125). This brilliant añejo is the color of a Hawaiian sunrise and tastes like dulce de leche spread on an apple wedge. There's some spice to it as well, but it balances the sweetness rather than overwhelms it. The 1942 is aged at least two and a half years in American white-oak barrels, and made with the company's most exclusive distillate. This goes without saying in good company, but I'll say it anyway as there may be cretins among us—Don Julio 1942 should never be polluted with margarita mix, nor is it to be slammed down the gullet frat-boy style. This is primo stuff best served in a snifter and enjoyed one delectable sip at a time. 1942 is a tequila sixty-plus years in the making; it deserves a few moments of your time.

---

* "Why pay more for a woody?" would make for a great commercial hook, wouldn't it?

† Spanish for "legalized sweatshops."

° Ditto for this one on the Google front.

best way to enjoy tequila. Really, I did. For real. My Spanish is limited to asking directions to the toilet and ordering shitty beer, so it took a great deal of effort to discover that there's more to tequila than meets the margarita. Eventually, with the help of a most affable and adorable translator, I procured what I was after from a local bartender who attested that real Mexicans love the Vampiro, a combination of tequila, lime juice or Squirt soda, and sangrita. He even mixed one up for me, which I found to be *muy excelente* . . . especially if you want to keep it real.

"Eez a reeel frog, man," the Mexican shop owner volunteered as I surveyed the contents of a makeshift display case. On a trip in which I'd encountered more than a few twisted items, the shellacked, conga-playing dead frog was by far the most peculiar. So I bought it . . . for eight dollars.

"You should've bought the whole band," Bottomfeeder said later at the bar La Cava, a squalid watering hole in Nogales and the nerve center for my Bandera-Vampiro research. He was referring to the saxophone-, bass-, and drum-playing shellacked dead frogs the shop also offered for sale. Without a lead singer, though, I figured it was pointless. Tossing back a stiff shot of tequila, I told Bottomfeeder as much.

"Fuckin' singers," he mumbled. Then he swallowed each color of the flag in rapid succession. I noted, for the record, that he looked oddly at home in Mexico. And he didn't seem at home in many places. But somewhere in the fifteenth hour of the drive from Santa Monica, I'd decided the entire road trip would be the stuff of a highly investigative junket that could be legitimately expensed to my employer. So, for the record, let me note that subsequent research revealed that in her compelling tome *The Complete Frog: A Guide for the Very Young Naturalist*, Elizabeth Lacey wrote that, "Because frogs are so delicious to so many efficient hunters, it is not surprising to learn that their lives are seldom very long." Nowhere in her book, however, did she mention the number of frogs whose lives are cut short only to become freak collectibles.

I suppose that Elizabeth Lacey never hauled her ass down to Nogales. If she had, she would have discovered that mutilated frogs are by no means the only bizarre goods for sale in the dusty Mexican border town. In fact, it's safe to say that just about everything and everybody in Nogales is for sale, including goodies such as bathroom-tiled night tables, authentic Mexican ponchos embroidered with— what else?—NFL logos, wood-carved field mice, and the town's best-selling item, uncut vanilla. What I'm ever going to do with a five-gallon drum of vanilla I have no idea. But I've got one simply because I was able to haggle the price down to twenty dollars, which is what a trip to Nogales is all about: the exhilaration of haggling for worthless goods and services you'd otherwise never dream of owning. In Nogales, haggling is the quintessential form of social contact and can earn the most diligent shoppers either the utmost respect or the utter disdain of the people they deal with. More important, haggling affords you the opportunity to say things like, "How much for that seven-foot-tall, wood-carved Blessed Mother?"

"Seekstee-five dollars?"

"I'll give you twenty."

"Forty-five."

"Twenty-five."

"Thirty."

"Hah! I'll take it." It was as if I'd stolen the perfect Christmas gift for my mother right out from under that shady son-of-a-bitch's nose. It was only later that I realized that all I'd come away with was a rather grotesque and inordinately heavy religious bauble that would almost certainly spell the end of my mother/son relationship if I ever chose to ship it back home to Philadelphia. And it was no easy task, mind you, negotiating the crowded streets of Nogales saddled with a shellacked, conga-playing dead frog; a five-gallon drum of pure, uncut vanilla; a seven-foot, wood-carved Blessed Mother; and Bottomfeeder, who'd thrown back one too many shots of tequila. I enlisted the help of a young Mexican boy so slight that his baseball cap seemed to weigh him down. But he was eager and shamefully poor, so I let him carry the frog, a sympathetic gesture I thought might give me a needed karma boost somewhere down the line.

"That's all?" he cried incredulously as I handed him a five-dollar bill, which, in my estimation, was more than ample payment for carrying a dead frog a mere two blocks. "Gringo tacaño!" he yelled before dropping the frog, kicking me in the shin, and taking off with my money, vanishing instantly into the crowded street.

Bottomfeeder shrugged, then motioned toward a decrepit old donkey inexplicably covered with black paint splotches: a most unusual photo opportunity, to say the least. "You need a picture with the painted burro," he declared. "It'll help you capture the true Mexican flavor." I was already convinced that vanilla was the true Mexican flavor, but running agonizingly low on culturally enhancing options,

I gingerly climbed aboard the old burro—Hector was his name—
ridiculously attired in a sombrero and multicolored serape. Sitting
astride Hector, posing for a Polaroid, I finally understood why,
despite Bottomfeeder's objections, I'd taken a detour through
Nogales. First off, it was par for our journey, which had evolved into
one big detour that included stopovers in Tombstone, Oklahoma
City, and New Orleans. But at that particular moment it felt right
because I was a footloose American in a Mexican den of depravity,
and I'd come, I'd seen, and I'd haggled, even if my efforts to barter
away the seven-foot-tall, wood-carved Blessed Mother for the
Polaroid proved futile.

"Four dollars," the photographer demanded as Hector looked
away impassively.

"But this statue is worth sixty-five. I'll trade you straight up."

"No, señor."

"The vanilla?"

"Noooooo, señor."

"How about the frog, then?" I implored.

The vendor looked long and hard at my musically attuned
amphibian, then shook his head and countered, "*No lo quiero, sin el
cantante.*"

"What did he say?" I asked Bottomfeeder, who had surprised me
with, among other things, his proficiency in Spanish.

"He said, 'I don't want it without the singer.'"

Fuckin' singers, I thought. "Let's get the hell out of here."

♦ ♇ ♉ ♇ ♦

It was on another trip to Mexico, sans Bottomfeeder, in the town of Arandas in the highlands of Jalisco, that I was introduced to Tezon, quite possibly the smoothest tequila on the market today.* The impeccable flavor of Tezon is a direct result of a high level of crafts-manship. It's made from 100 percent blue agave that is quartered, brick-oven roasted, and then crushed by a traditional "Tahona" mill-stone, a giant wheel fashioned from volcanic rock. Unlike most dis-tillers, the makers of Tezon do not discard the pulped agave fibers after grinding, opting instead to leave the pulp in the juice through fermentation and the first of two distillations. Crystal-clear Tezon blanco, which is bottled immediately, is the purest expression of the agave, while the reposado and añejo tequilas are aged a bit in seasoned white-oak barrels.

A hundred miles to the west of Arandas, nestled at the base of a volcano, is the tiny town of Tequila, ground zero for the production of the agave-based potable first distilled by ancient Aztec tribesmen. Over the past twenty-five years in the United States, tequila has evolved from being primarily the unrefined hootch of choice of shot-silly college students on spring break to a top-shelf spirit that competes with single-malt Scotches and premium vodkas for the hearts and taste buds of sophisticated tipplers with fat wallets. The town of Tequila is home to Jose Cuervo, the world's best-selling tequila. I once

---

* Of course, "today"—the one in which I'm typing these words—is February 27, 2007. By the time this tome reaches your hands—and the hands of everyone on your Christmas list—a host of new premium tequilas will have likely appeared. That's why plans are already in the works for a follow-up to this book, tentatively titled, *Nobody Likes a Quitter 2: Electric Boogaloo.*

attended a lavish fiesta at Cuervo headquarters in celebration of the release of the 2004 Reserva de la Familia—the brand's premium añejo. The party was totally off the hook, with several hundred jaw-dropping Latinas slinking around in tiny dresses that were virtually painted on. None of them wanted anything to do with me, of course, no doubt because I was the only goofball there wearing a white linen suit.*

I ended up making time with—you guessed it—a publicist from Newport Beach named Brooklyn. She worked for an agency that represented Cuervo, and joked† that she was only hanging out with me because her boss had asked her to make sure I had a good time.

"I'm a team player," Brooklyn quipped before swallowing half a glass of tequila as though it were a Jell-O shot. Before long, I discovered she really meant it, too. Team player? Hell, that lush-ous lady was MVP of the Orange County Sloppy Drunks.

We went back to my hotel room in the hopes of finding some common ground to build upon, and find some we did—in the form of those engaging fleshy lumps known as breasts and the blood-filled rod called . . . well, you get the idea. Problem was, beyond the boobs and boner, all we were left with were the not-nearly-so-engaging list-less lumps known as each other. Not to mention the number Brooklyn did on my neck. Remember when getting a hickey was just the coolest thing in the world? It was like the pubescent equivalent of

---

* That's the last time I ever accept fashion advice from my mother, who still wears pastel blazers with shoulder pads from the 1984 Linda Evans collection.

† At least, I *think* she was joking.

a diamond bracelet or a dozen long-stemmed roses. Indeed, a well-placed hickey served notice to every kid in school that, hey, not only does someone *like* me, she likes me enough to suck on my throat 'til I bruise. Ah, young love—it really is something. It's another thing altogether, however, to wake up after a one-night stand in Mexico to find a conspicuously large blotch just below your chin line. Particularly when you're scheduled, as I was, to have lunch with the CEO of one of the world's largest spirits companies.

"I've never done this before," Brooklyn confided, snuggling beside me in bed as I weighed the perspiration factor of wearing a turtleneck in July against the embarrassment of explaining the ugly suck mark on my neck.

"What's that?" I muttered.

"Slept with a writer on a work trip," she said. "This is my first time."

"Congratulations!" I replied. My clumsy stab at humor was intended to throw her off balance, as I sensed that the conversation had moved into uncomfortable terrain. Sure enough, it had.

"Have you?" she asked.

"Have I what? Huh? Hey, are you hungry? Let's go grab a *taquito* somewhere, okay?"

"C'mon. You can tell me," she persisted. "Have you ever slept with a publicist on a work trip? Be honest."

"Honestly," I stalled, running Bill Clinton–like over my not-quite-lying responses. I could deny based on the use of the term "sleep," or on the fact that my memory is so faulty that lying is always suspect, or deny that what I do could be honestly described as "work." But then I just lied like a man, "I haven't, either. You popped my publicist cherry."

She eyed me skeptically, but I held her gaze like the seasoned truth masseuse I have become. As is so often the case when one finds oneself naked with a stranger in a strange land, a certain politician-in-an-election-year-type ethics was in order. Hey, voters *need* to be lied to. Euphemistically speaking, in exchange for her vote Brooklyn wanted me to promise to cut her taxes *and* increase funding for social services. This is akin to the incessant spew of bullshit that netted that swine George W. Bush eight years in the White House. Hell, I was a Clinton man—all I wanted was another roll in the hay.

"You're not lying, are you?"

"Absolutely not," I responded, wondering if she would wonder if that was a glib vodka reference, which come to think of it, maybe it should have been. "You asked if I've slept with any other publicists and I told you the God's honest truth—no sleep 'til Brooklyn."

The Beastie Boys quip made her smile. Needless to say, with all due respect to Mr. and Mrs. Clinton's lock on New York politics, that night the Beasties and I carried Brooklyn.

· ♀ ♥ ♀ ·

A strong argument could be made that I struck a bum deal in securing the rights to Bottomfeeder's life, but believe it or not there was a time when it looked as though he might prove my winning lottery ticket after all. That was back in 2005, when something implausible happened: Bottomfeeder became a leading man. In a movie. A REAL movie. Like most everything else that occurs in this fatuous fool's life, there was no rhyme or reason to his moment in the sun.

One minute he was leading a neighborhood protest of an intrusive film production; the next he was doing love scenes with Kirsten Dunst.* Nobody's been that lucky since Jed Clampett took that shot at the rabbit and struck bubbling crude.

"I was out there picketing, cuz I wanted them to stop shining those bright thingies outside my bedroom window all night long," Bottomfeeder explained while sipping on a triple-soy chai latte something-or-other.†

"They're called lights, man," I interjected.

"Huh?"

"Those 'thingies' are lights. Movie lights."

"Oh, yeah, whatever. So then the cops show up and start arresting everybody. It took three of 'em with pepper spray and billy clubs to subdue me—I've been working out, and all—but eventually they did, and next thing you know I'm being savagely beaten behind a squad car," he explained. He claims to have been rescued from the police by the producer of the film, a guy Bottomfeeder described as being "very powerful and Jewish." This producer said he liked Bottomfeeder's look. His LOOK?! What look would that be—Salvation Army chic? Skid row off-rack? Tommy Giveafinger?

"He says I have an 'old' Kieran Culkin thing going on," Bottom-feeder said between bites of a cucumber-and-bean-sprout-on-whole-

---

* Kirsten Dunst would most likely deny any knowledge of this and, in the interest of avoiding litigation, I would have to agree with her. Fully.

† Designer java, of course, is the First Stage of Official Hollywood Affectation (OHA).

grain-bread sandwich.* "And he thinks me and Kirsten generate real heat on-screen." At this point, I wanted to shake my fist at the heavens and scream, "Why God, why?" but instead found myself asking Bottomfeeder for more details about the project.

"It's called *Code Name: Mingus* and it's about this dashing international spy who kills lots of people and listens to jazz music. I play his sidekick, Remy."

"High concept," I said, or at least I think it was me who said it.

"*Really* high," he replied, "and they say it has huge European potential. We're doing the opening in Montreal this winter."†

I nodded numbly. Why? I don't know for sure. I just did. Maybe the notion of Bottomfeeder becoming the next Ben Affleck or Brad Pitt was so unsettling, so patently absurd, that hearing about it short-circuited that part of my brain that would otherwise generate an appropriate response, such as a regurgitation. So I nodded, and continued to nod as Bottomfeeder spewed other nonsense like, "My agent thinks the role is good for me at this critical juncture in my career," and, "I hope you won't mind making yourself scarce later, dude. Kirsten's coming over to run lines."

Later, as I paced about on the street outside my building while they rehearsed, I began to put things into perspective. A bigger man would have found joy in his friend's good fortune. A better man would have offered to help out, maybe by talking to mutual friends

---

* Stage Two of OHA

† *Code Name: Mingus* was never released. Or made, for that matter. And Kirsten Dunst is still way hot, even if neither I nor anyone I know has ever met her.

about dropping certain restraining orders. But this man was thinking of a certain attorney on the Westside code-named "the Beast" who makes a cruel living off casually written talent contracts. I was thinking my five-hundred-dollar investment might turn out to be a bigger boon than anything I had invested in during the heady dot-com days. As for Bottomfeeder, well, so what if PETA got pissed about inhumane treatment of that dumb animal?

• ♀ ♥ ♀ •

"You know the best thing about being a movie star?" Bottomfeeder wondered aloud as he lounged on my sofa drinking my tequila,* eating my food, and watching my television. "The parking, that's what."

Parking, huh? That was certainly news to me. I figured the best thing about being a movie star was freeloading, since Bottomfeeder—who had inexplicably emerged as a Hollywood semiplayer—seemed to enjoy nothing more than lying around my apartment, consuming my things. He'd been at it, rent-free, for nearly four years. "Look at this," he continued, pointing to an apparent movie on the TV. "Affleck's headed to a meeting in the middle of Manhattan, and there's

---

* I was introduced to Corzo tequila in the summer of '05 while partying at the hillside Santa Monica abode of actor Luke Wilson, star of such memorable movies as *Old School*, *Legally Blonde*, and *The Royal Tenenbaums*. Luke also appeared in *Alex & Emma* and the 2004 remake of *Around the World in 80 Days*, but after about the third or fourth time I brought those clunkers up, I got the distinct impression he'd rather forget them. I mention Luke Wilson partly because he turned me on to a very enjoyable tequila, but mainly because I want to drop as many names as possible in this book in the hope that people will find me interesting. You have *your* ambitions; I have mine.

a spot right there in front of the building. He didn't even have to par-allel park because the whole freakin' street was clear. Unbelievable! I mean, tell me, when does that ever happen in real life?"

"Not very often," I muttered, resisting the urge to point out that Hollywood movies generally have about as much in common with real life as, well, Bottomfeeder's life does. It was then, to my great dismay, that I noticed he'd drained the last of the Corzo.*

"I'm gonna call my agent and tell him I need to have prime parking like that in my next movie," Bottomfeeder suddenly shouted. "Did I tell you? I'm working with Triple H and Steven Seagal in a comedy about three guys who get stuck caring for a little baby girl."

See what I mean?

"So you're doing a remake," I said.

"Huh?"

"A remake. Of *Three Men and a Baby*."

This drew a blank stare from Bottomfeeder.

"It's a movie from the '80s. Tom Selleck, Ted Danson, and Steve Guttenberg. Same storyline. I think Leonard Nimoy directed it."

---

* Corzo distinguishes itself from other premium tequilas with a patented "heart of hearts" produc-tion process that involves three distillations and requires more than double the usual amount of blue agave per bottle. What's unique about the process is that Corzo is redistilled *after* aging for several months in white-oak barrels, a more aggressive approach to eradicating the "heads and tails" (the undesirable parts of a distillate). Corzo also employs a technique called "sparging," the introduction before bottling of air bubbles that allow the tequila to breathe. What it all amounts to is one of the more refined tequilas on the market, and with an elegant bottle created by acclaimed designer Fabien Baron, Corzo looks as good on the bar as it tastes in a glass.

"Spock? Directed?"

I nodded.

"Wow, that's weird," he said. "Cuz the baby in this movie turns out to be a flesh-eating alien just like those little furry things on *Star Trek*. It goes on a killing rampage and me, Triple H, and Seagal have to stop it."

"It sounds intense," I said, having no clue what else I possibly *could* say to that.

"Yeah, it is," he replied. "There's this one scene where the baby . . . uh, alien . . . whatever, kills this drifter played by the lead singer of Better Than Ezra. It is without a doubt the goriest scene ever committed to celluloid. Just awesome!"

"Wait, the guy from Better Than Ezra is in your movie?"

"Of course he is,"* Bottomfeeder replied without a hint of irony. Then he began shaking the remote control like a Yoo-hoo from Hell. "Hey, I think this thing might need new batteries."

At that, Restraint got up and stormed out the door. "You know, brutha, YOU could go out and get batteries. In fact, YOU could even pay for them. Because the only guy who ever uses it is YOU. YOU. YOU. YOU! YOU!! YOU!!!"

"What are you trying to say?" he asked.

"I'm saying maybe our little arrangement has run its course. Our series is not getting picked up. Our option has expired. Principal photography is cancelled. You're eighty-sixed. Your next movie, *Exit City*.

---

* He wasn't.

The sequel, *Scram-O* . . . look, I agreed to let you crash on the couch for a few months because I owed your uncle—my landlord—some money from that grease-fire thing. But that was, like, four years ago, and you're not poor anymore . . . at least, not financially."

Bottomfeeder looked at me with a flicker of interest. "You want me to move out? Sorry, bro, but no can do. My acting coach says at this point in my career I need to keep it real, hang with the Real People, keep doing what I'm doing, you know. Evicted? From here? Man, the press would have a field day. So maybe later, dude."

And with that he got up, grabbed the five-thousand-dollar bicycle the studio had sent over, muttered something about being out of brews, and banged the tires against both sides of the doorway as he left. "Later," he said. "Gotta get a ride in before *McCloud* comes on." And I was left staring into space. Parking, indeed.

Step 5

Getting Boozy . . . and the Beast

Nobody seems really certain if the Beast—the famous and tempestuous SoCal attorney I attempted to retain to protect my interests in the life of the suddenly celebritized Bottomfeeder—has "666" tattooed on his inner thigh. But I have it on good authority that the Mr. Wolf character in *Pulp Fiction* is based on him . . . and it's also rumored that the Beast paid a fancy East Coast PR Firm $250,000 to get the rumor started. The Beast's specialty is contract law, palimony cases, and common-law tort. One of his signature techniques is getting beauties to roam about the town during their "fertile time" and hit up wealthy guys in a quest to develop a paternity situation; the Beast calls it "supply-side paternity payout." Another Beastly tactic: he takes opposing counsel out for drinks to talk about a settlement, then has the parking lot attendant remove a taillight from the guy's Jaguar. Later, he reports the car to the DUI hotline claiming to have witnessed "a nut in a Jag driving a hundred miles an hour without one of his back lights and nearly running over children." Of course, in the morning, the DUI stays private provided the settlement gets made.

It took some time to find the Beast, who turned out to be lunching with three expectant sirens beside the Beverly Hilton pool. I informed him that reaching his abode had cost me three bartender bribes, and would not have been necessary had he simply returned my repeated phone calls to the 800 number I found scrawled in blood across a bathroom mirror. He pressed a button next to a scrumptious-looking pitcher of **sangria** and two uniformed geeks appeared from nowhere; as they gently lifted me by my armpits, the Beast informed me that earlier that very day he'd been retained by none other than my roomie, aka the Bottomfeeder, who inexplicably found his name and number inside a matchbox that somebody had dropped in Aspen's famed J-Bar.

"Sangria" derives from the Spanish word for "blood," and it says here that vampires ain't got nothing on the Spaniards, besides the

---

⚡ Sangria Is Bloody Good ⚡

My love affair with sangria began many years ago in Spain, during Seville's amazing Feria de Abril, a nonstop weeklong bash widely considered the most bacchanalian event on the city's social calendar. My days were spent perfecting the Sevillana, a distinctly Andalusian form of flamenco dancing, the nights reserved for sipping sweet wine punch in the private *caseta* of an alluring Spanish socialite who'd somehow gotten the impression I was an important member of the international spirits media. It was an impressive connection indeed, considering the socialite didn't understand a lick of English and the closest I'd ever come to speaking a foreign language was uttering the words, "Of course I really love you."

continued on next page >>

Sangria

1 orange, sliced thin
1 lemon, sliced thin
2 tablespoons superfine granulated sugar
1 bottle chilled dry red wine
1/2 cup cognac
1/4 cup Grand Marnier
2 tablespoons orange juice
1 cup chilled seltzer or club soda

In a bowl, muddle the orange and lemon slices with the sugar. Add red wine, cognac, Grand Marnier, and orange juice. Stir until sugar is dissolved. Transfer to a punch bowl, chill overnight, then stir in seltzer, add plenty of ice, and serve.

ability to tap a jugular vein, that is. There are countless recipes for sangria, and my favorite mix comes courtesy of the Food Network, which ranks up there with Spike and Animal Planet among the most useful channels on basic cable.

"What's Bottomfeeder doing in Aspen?" I asked incredulously.

"The Caller ID would indicate he's staying out at Eisner's place . . . he said with Kirsten Dunst, I think . . . or maybe it's Kirstie Ally . . . something with a 'K' in it." One of the preggo chicks was distracting the Beast by rubbing tanning lotion all over his enormous, hairy belly.

Bottomfeeder? At Michael Eisner's place? With a *woman?* A famous woman, no less? Surely, the Beast was mad. Or perhaps he was lying in an effort to jack up his already exorbitant fees. Besides, why on earth would Bottomfeeder need an attorney?

"You know that contract between you guys?" growled the

Beast. "The one that says you own the rights to my client's life story?"

I nodded suspiciously.

"Well," the Beast continued, "it ain't worth the napkin it's scribbled on."

"Says who?" I countered, feeling hot blood rush to my cheeks and suddenly resenting being held aloft by the two geeks.

"Says me! Thing is, buddy-boy, my client signed the contract while under duress, possibly under the influence of adult beverages, and very likely under the threat of bodily harm, which could be kidnapping in California . . . but he's a nice guy, which is why I'm not asking that you be arrested on federal charges, but only petitioning the court to render the napkin null and void."

"Duress?"

"That's right, duress. And fear of imminent bodily harm."

"*Of course* he was under duress," I shouted. "A bookie was going to kill him unless he came up with five hundred dollars. So I gave him the money in exchange for the rights to his life. A theretofore totally meaningless life that I saved!"

"Look, there's no reason to get excited," the Beast practically whispered, his voice suddenly softer than Michael Moore's abs. He nodded and the geeks set me down gently. "Why don't we head into the hotel bar?" he cooed. "We'll have a few **limoncellos** and see if we can come to some sort of settlement. You're parked with the valet, right?"

A taillight on my car went missing, and shortly thereafter I found myself behind the eight ball at the bargaining table. It took everything

❧ Like Lemonade for Big People ❧

Limoncello is a fresh-tasting liqueur made from sun-kissed Mediterranean lemons, sugar, and alcohol that has been a staple in the Old Country for generations. My favorite labels have long been Villa Massa and Limoncello di Capri, but in recent years I've taken a shine to Limoncé—Italy's number-one-selling brand. One of my favorite limoncello concoctions, the Belmont Gran Centennial, was created by talented New York mixologist Aviram Turgeman a few years back in celebration of the hundredth anniversary of the famed New York racetrack.

The Belmont Gran Centennial

0.75 oz. GranGala Triple Orange Liqueur
0.75 oz. Limoncé limoncello
1.5 oz. Bacardi Limón rum
0.5 oz. fresh lime juice
1.5 oz. Brut champagne
lemon verbena sprig for garnish

Pour first four ingredients into a mixing glass, add ice, and shake for six seconds; strain into an ice-filled highball glass. Top off with the champagne. Garnish with the lemon verbena and serve with two long sipping straws.

I had to keep from resorting to violence, something the Beast—whose firm also handles personal injury suits—would have surely welcomed. Fortunately, I would get a brief reprieve from the Beast-Bottomfeeder madness in the form of an all-expenses-paid junket to the Great White North, a place that has not only given the world some of its biggest stars (Jim Carrey, Pam Anderson, William Shatner, Loverboy), but is also a veritable cornucopia of alcohol-related delights.

• ♉ ♉ ♉ •

Despite my impassioned appeal to reconsider what I deemed to be her rather close-minded position, the bondage-diva security officer at LAX was adamant in her belief that Canada is some sort of sovereign nation—*not* our fifty-first state—and insisted that I produce proper identification in order to fly there. "Besides a Costco card!" she growled, clearly unaware of just how difficult it is to obtain Super Saver status in these troubled times. "You need to show me a passport or a birth certificate within twenty minutes, or else you aren't getting on that plane. Got it?"

So as you can see, my trip to the Great White North didn't start off so well. Not that I was overly worried, mind you. Years of working as a writer on the go had inured me to the gamut of indignities regularly visited upon weary travelers by obstinate airport employees. So when one of Alaska Airlines' finest brazenly rejected my savings club card as "worthless," well, I simply flashed her a wicked grin suggesting that not only was I the sort who might allow a stranger to pack my bags for me, but that I'd also flat-out lie about it at the check-in counter.*

Calls were made to well-connected associates at the FAA, and before you could say "Barenaked Ladies rule!" I was on my way to Vancouver, a city I knew embarrassingly little about, save that (a) Mick Jagger once hailed it as the best strip-club city in the world, and (b) so did my cousin Fonzo from Jersey. It turns out there's lots to do

---

* This is a risky strategy best left to professional travel liars; miss the mark and you will never casually associate the word "cavity" with dentistry again.

in Vancouver besides stuff funny-looking money into the G-strings of well-endowed women. It truly is, as the Official Visitors' Guide claims, "a special place where the mountains melt into the shore, and where wild rivers rush to meet the ocean." And, I might add, a place where the strippers will let you keep their underwear if you ask nicely enough. Boy, was Jagger ever right about the place.

I stayed at an über-trendy boutique hotel called Opus, a converted warehouse on Davie Street in the Yaletown section of the city. Opus, by all accounts, was at the time *the* place to see and be seen in Vancouver, and I spent hours ogling its urbane denizens, along with a selection of celebs that included Michael Stipe, David Duchovny, and Sarah Michelle Gellar. Had a drunken Tommy Lee showed up and started hitting on the ladies, well, it would have been *exactly* like a night out at the Chateau Marmont in Hollywood. The ninety-seven-room Opus has five varying décor styles, named after fictional personality types such as "Mike," a New York doctor who drives a Saab and likes the muted palette of a loft-influenced suite (I'm not making this up, as if I could). I stayed in a "Susan," a tasteful room, according to the hotel's general manager, David Curell, designed for "a fashion analyst who likes Manolo Blahnik shoes." You will of course remember power forward and defensive specialist Manolo Blahnik from that playoff series when his Knicks bested the Celtics in six games.

"Perhaps you'd prefer a 'Dede,'" Curell generously offered. "She's a method actor from L.A. who shops at Fred Segal." Well, given that I'm a wannabe screenwriter who knows several L.A. songs and used to drive past Fred Segal on my way to perform safety inspections at the El Segundo slaughterhouse, Dede made more sense than Susan. But

I decided to stay put. Too bad they didn't have a "Fonzo," a paroled Teamster from Newark who beats people up for sport.

I was pleased to discover that each of the Opus Hotel's rooms came equipped with a Sony Playstation unit, not to mention an expansive selection of in-room adult entertainment with which to satisfy the ol' avaricious concupiscence. The most intriguing amenity, however, was the "Oxy-Gene"—a portable, handheld oxygen canister containing more than twelve minutes' worth of oxygen-enriched air. Ostensibly, sucking on this sleek little gadget will stimulate cells, kick-start the metabolism, and thereby provide for increased energy. But the real reason these babies were a hit at Opus is simple: a potent oxygen injection does wonders to relieve the sting of a wicked hangover. And if you're planning on hitting the town in party-crazed Vancouver, it's nice to know that "morning after" relief is only a few deep breaths away.

Of course, a report on Vancouver would not be complete without a mention of Brandi's, which offers the best "exotic entertainment" north of Snoop Dogg's crib. The dancers—most of whom have adopted luxury vehicle–inspired stage names—are beautiful, friendly, and best of all, COMPLETELY NUDE! Oh, Canada, thank you for being so uninhibited, so au naturel, so . . . so . . . poonielicious. That whole big mess a few years back, you know, with Iraq, and you not supporting us and all that? Well, you're forgiven. And you've got Lexus, Mercedes, and Portia (with a "T," like in Shakespeare) to thank for it.

By the time I got back to Susan at the Opus, things had begun to blur a bit in that delightful way familiar to those who have visited

World Class destinations with a decent press credential and the ethics one might expect from a second-generation Washington lobbyist on a three-week meth bender. My notes for the design of the newest Opus room, "Brandi," include a detailed leather budget and, in a large red scrawl, "MUST hire LAX security dominatrix as room designer" across the top of the page. Ah, Vancouver, cling to your damned independent ways and your play-money currency (how very French of you!) but know in your heart of hearts that some of us Down South will always associate you with a certain fifty-first state of mind. And you'll have me, Mick, and Fonzo to thank if there's ever a Brandi room at the Opus.

One week later, back in LA . . .

"I hope there are no hard feelings about, you know, the whole THING with the lawyer and all," Bottomfeeder said matter-of-factly between the final bites of a leftover Shakey's pizza, which he washed down with a Tiger beer.*

"Hard feelings? About the THING?" I replied. "Oh, you must mean the THING where you hired a professional purloiner called the Beast to sue ME—the guy whose sofa you've been sleeping on rent-free all these years—for 'criminal negligence' and 'emotional damage' caused by my 'egregious failure' to keep the refrigerator adequately stocked with beer and Hot Pockets? No, man, why would I still be

---

* Imported from Singapore, where it is that country's best-selling brew, Tiger Beer first made contact with Western palates during World War II, when it became the thirst-quencher of choice for Allied forces serving in the region.

mad about that? After all, the ink's been dry on that diktat for nearly a week!!!"

"Cool," Bottomfeeder said as he cracked open my last bottle of beer. "And by the way, we're out of Flying Dog. And did I tell ya what a great time Kirsten Dunst and I had in Aspen? That place freakin' rocks, dude. You should go back for a visit . . . once you, um, get back on your feet financially and stuff."

"You don't say?" I did say, while weighing the long-term "emotional damage" I might suffer over the course of a long prison sentence versus the immediate intoxication I'd surely experience were I to manslaughter the "egregious failure" who was riffling through my CD collection.

"Yep. Lots of chicks and mountains and shit. And Eisner flew out for the weekend and took us to dinner at a place called Condiments or Condoms and Drums . . . I dunno, something with a 'C' in it . . . and then we went dancing at Scooters and then Mike signed me to a three-picture deal with points on the back end. My agent says we scored big-time, and Kirsten bought me a new Jag."

My mood was foul as I trudged through the grocery store pushing a cart loaded with more Tiger beer and Hot Pockets. The Bottom-feeder situation had gone from unpleasant to calamitous—he was getting rich and famous, apparently sleeping with Kirsten Dunst, and was legally entitled to half (which wasn't much) of everything I owned. On top of that, he'd made it clear that despite his newfound prosperity, he had no plans to move out of my apartment. "I like the mise-en-scène of the place," he told me. "Keepin' it real, dude." I eyed the fine edge of a kitchen knife in the utensils aisle as he continued: "Plus, I'm much more comfortable now that I'm in the bedroom instead of on the couch. By the way, when do you think you'll have the rest of your stuff outta there?"

Browsing in the magazine and paperbacks aisle, I considered buying a copy of Norman Vincent Peale's *The Power of Positive Thinking*. But then I thought, *What the hell good would that do?*

Oh, and before we move on to the next chapter—and lest you think things couldn't have gotten any worse for me—check out the following e-mail exchange:

Date: Tuesday, October 5th

To: Dan Dunn

From: Barry Silver, 20th Century Fox Television

Re: "Polly's Pros" pilot notes

Dear Dan:

Hope you're having a fantastic day. Is this weather we've been having simply fantastic or what? Fisher tells me you've been doing some traveling. Hope you're keeping out of trouble, you wild man (ha, ha!).

Anyhoo, we received your latest draft of the "Polly's Pros" pilot script, and while we're certainly pleased that you finally got around to making some revisions, I must tell you that we still have some significant concerns about the overall direction and tone of the work. I respect the fact that, as Fisher regularly assures us, you're an artist who is fiercely protective of your own unique vision, but truth be told, some folks here at the network are interpreting your "chutzpah" and complete disregard of our notes to be somewhat of a disobliging attitude. Don't get me wrong, Dan, we here at Fox are still very excited about this partnership with you and look forward to all the fantastic things the future holds, but in the interest of ensuring that "Polly's Pros" makes it into the prime-time lineup, we graciously ask for a little more effort from you to meet us halfway on our requests. For instance, when we pointed out that the "Squeeze my tits" catchphrase was in violation of FCC decency standards, we assumed you'd revise accordingly. I don't think I need to tell you that "Eat shit, bitch!" is not an acceptable alternative, yet for some baffling reason, that's just what you offered in the rewrite. What's wrong with my suggestions—"Pinch my buns," "Whatever!" and "Fluff off, toots!"? Based on extensive focus-group testing, we're confident that any one of those will resonate with viewers. Also, we noticed that in the latest draft, you inexplicably opted to change the story line from Polly trying to convince her unsuspecting mother that the brothel she runs is a nunnery, to a decidedly unfunny scenario that has her being savagely beaten by Colombian drug dealers. We can only assume that this is some kind of misguided joke, Dan, as you cannot really believe that 20th Century Fox would ever produce a sitcom about a "smack-addicted whore," as you brazenly retitled the pilot. To make matters worse, an understandably distraught Tracy Nelson is threatening to pull out of the entire project. Please get back to me ASAP with your thoughts on these matters. We'd very much like to resolve and move forward. Okay? Fantastic.

—Barry

I responded a week later. . . .

BS:

Yep, I have been traveling. Or at least I was until some overzealous pig pulled me over for a broken taillight last week in Utah and the shit hit the fan. Goddamn outstanding bench warrants! Nothing FAN-TASTIC about spending a week in the pokey sharing a cell with an ornery three-hundred-pound guy named Big Dread, Barry, that's for damn sure. The only reason you're getting this reply is because the turnkey at the Green River County Jail failed to probe my ass for the Blackberry. So, for obvious reasons, I gotta make this quick. The reason I altered the pilot the way I did was cuz God spoke to me in a dream and told me to do so. That's right—the Big Man Himself wants us to use this sitcom as His vessel in a crusade against social injustice, and He vowed to smite anyone who stands in the way of the good work we're doing. Therefore, it's imperative that Polly remain a smack-addicted whore *and* die a grotesque and painful death at the end of the first episode. This will send the appropriate messages to the masses: drugs and sex are bad, and Tracy Nelson is the Antichrist. Big Dread thinks we're a lock for an Emmy nomination. I've hired him to be the assistant head writer for the series. We're putting the finishing touches on the second-episode script right now. Don't want to ruin the surprise ending, but let's just say the slaying of an abortion doctor has never been funnier. Also, Barry, it would be a big help if you could post bail for Big Dread and me. The food here is not very good.

Fluff off, toots!

—DD

His reply arrived in thirty-seven seconds. . . .

Dan:

We're passing on "Polly's Pros." You need professional help.

—Barry

Step 6

You Know What They Say About
Guys with Small Chapters . . .

We were dead at Fox, and everyone from Polly Holliday to Tracy
Nelson to Nick Lachey's personal trainer's assistant was threatening
to sue me, so Fisher really had to earn his 10 percent of nothing to get
me another meeting in town. It wound up being at MTV, where I met
with a twenty-two-year-old African-American development exec
named Blake Shipley to discuss an idea I had for a reality TV show
called *Ride My Pimp!*—sort of like *The Amazing Race* meets HBO's
Hookers and Johns. Fisher thought the idea had legs, and that there'd be
ample opportunity for promotional tie-ins . . . mostly from gun man-
ufacturers and pharmaceutical companies that specialize in penicillin.

I recall being excited when I learned that Blake Shipley was
black, because at that time, in yet another misguided attempt at bet-
tering myself, I'd taken to incorporating "street" jargon into everyday
conversation. I'd found that when dealing with, say, some of the
more youthful magazine editors or folks from the entertainment
industry, simply tossing in a few words and expressions co-opted

from hip underprivileged youth really added extra validity, or "cred" as they say in the giddyack, to whatever message I was attempting to convey. Fo-sniffle! Then again, I also found that it didn't always work out that way.

"We hired a market research firm to evaluate the show's prospects, and the results of a comprehensive study were extremely encouraging, especially in the highly coveted eighteen- to thirty-four-year-old male demographic," I told Blake, adding, "and the concept is the shiz-nit, bee-otch!"

"Excuse me?" Blake said.

"You know . . . the shiz-nit. Abracadabra. Crescent fresh as all get out. Dope. Da Bomb."

"I'm sorry, but I'm not quite following," said Blake, his gaze drifting from my FUBU skully down to the brand-new Malcolm X T-shirt I'd worn for the occasion.

"The doo-doo. Phat. The goot," I continued. "Off the hook. Super saucy. The kind of show that will really bring in the advertisers, so that you and I will be rolling in the luchini. I'm talkin' mad stacks to the fullest."

"The what?"

"The benjamins. The downs. Dead presidents. Bones."

"Look, can you just tell me, in as straightforward a manner as possible, what this show is about? What happens in a typical episode?"

"Okay, we got these pimps—outgoing, photogenic pimps with great personalities. And they'll be carrying prostitutes on their backs in a series of timed challenges . . . like racing against each other . . .

away from the cops, gangbangers, et cetera. Plus, to amp up the drama, all the contestants will be living together in the same house. A crack house."

"Pimps and hookers running around a crack house. And you want us to put this on MTV?"

I nodded enthusiastically.

"Is this some kind of joke?"

"Uh, well, there'll be some comedy, sure. But I see it as more of an action-thriller-suspense kind of reality program. I don't think that's been attempted before."

"With pimps and hookers?"

"We don't have to call them that, if that's an issue," I reassured Blake. "We could go with juggalos and hizzos, for instance."

"Look," he said. "We're not interested, and furthermore I really don't appreciate you coming in here and—"

"What's the dilly, yo? Why you playa hatin'? You some kinda bosepheus or something?"

"Bosepheus?"

"Yeah, you know, a brutha who has no funk. Much like Carlton on *The Fresh Prince*, this brutha is said to have 'honky' tendencies."

"Who you callin' a honky, wegro? I'm black!"

"Whoa, whoa, whoa, my man, be juggalo . . . keep it greasy. We cool," I told him. "There's no need for us to be griffin'. I wasn't trying to jank you or nuthin'. And besides, some of my best friends are black."

At this point an angry Blake, clearly envious of my superior ebonics skillz, pressed a button on his intercom and asked an assistant to summon security. Having been in similar situations before, I knew it was time to vamoose.

"Man, I don't get why you're so angry," I said with one leg already out the window. "You didn't happen to talk with Barry Silver from Fox recently, did you?"

"Just get out, man. Please!"

"Word," I replied. And with that, I was jailtrottin' down the street. I decided then and there that I was done swallowing my pride just to make it in Hollywood.* After all, I had a hell of a career going already. So what if script doctors and television-series creators made more scratch than a rabid cat in a flea-dip commercial? I got paid to get potted and tell people about it. Who *wouldn't* want a job like mine? Aside, that is, from people in AA, those poor bastards on the waiting list for liver transplants, and anyone interested in living past fifty?

Jeah, boy-eeeeeee!!!!!!

. ♆ ♇ ♆ .

When I got home I shared the news of my showbiz emancipation with Bottomfeeder, who greeted me with all the enthusiasm of a kid who'd been routinely denied entry to the candy store. It was 11:15 AM and he'd been up all night parked in front of the television drinking **Chambord** straight from the bottle and surfing the

---

* I also decided not to share that information with Fisher.

twenty-four-hour news channels. It'd been days since he'd showered, spoken, or even moved off the living room sofa, distraught over having been beaten out for a role in an upcoming David Lynch film by the kid who played Bud Bundy on *Married . . . with Children*. It was not an ideal time to engage Bottomfeeder in conversation—but then again, when was it ever?

⚔ The Spirit of Dead French Royalty ⚔

Louis XIV discovered Chambord in 1685 not long before he and his French army lay siege to Philipsburg. Somewhat coincidentally, I discovered the very same raspberry liqueur three hundred years later while laying siege to my parents' liquor cabinet in Philly after a high school dance. Louis XIV and his court were quite fond of the stuff and it quickly became the liqueur of choice of the French aristocracy. I, on the other hand, wasn't so enamored with Chambord at first, mainly because my prom date threw up on me after drinking it. The lesson here, kids: raspberry liqueur does not pair well with Natty Light, pure grain alcohol, and the semicaustic vocal stylings of Mr. Mister.

Since then I've come to appreciate Chambord for its distinct flavor and versatility. I'm also happy to report that Mr. Mister's "Broken Wings" has gotten less awful with age and that I can still hold my liquor better than most teenaged girls. Plus, the empty Chambord bottle I've got hanging from my rearview mirror looks mos' def. It has been called the quintessential cocktail ingredient, thanks to its uncanny knack for mixing well with almost anything (see above paragraph for exceptions). Here then, some raspberry-flavored treat recipes:

La Bohème
1 shot vodka
1/2 shot elderflower cordial
1/2 shot Chambord
1 1/2 shots cranberry juice

Shake all with ice and strain into a martini glass.

continued on next page >>

French Kiss
2 shots vodka
1 1/2 shots Chambord
1 shot white crème de cacao
1 shot heavy cream

Shake all with ice and strain into a martini glass. Float a mini Hershey's Kiss on top.

Raspberry Mochatini
1 shot espresso
1 1/2 shots raspberry vodka
3/4 shot brown crème de cacao
3/4 shot Chambord

Shake all with ice and strain into a martini glass. Garnish with shaved chocolate.

"Everything okay?" I asked delicately, so as not to agitate him further.

"Well, first off, fuck David Faustino," he spat. "That midget couldn't act his way out of a paper bag . . . and what does that mean, anyway? In what scenario would acting ability be necessary as a means of escaping from a bag?"

I nodded and said nothing, having learned from experience that it is best to remain silent whenever Bottomfeeder begins arguing figures of speech with himself. On the television, California's Governor Terminator was delivering a "state of the State" address in which he vowed to weed out the special interests he claimed were compromising the integrity of the legislative process.

"Yeah," Bottomfeeder barked. "And by 'special interests,' he means the interests of people who disagree with him. What a bunch of bullshit! They're all a bunch of fucking cocks, you know that?"

"Yep. Cocks," I said.

That exchange was followed by a rather lengthy lull in the conversation, in which Bottomfeeder picked at his skin and I tried unsuccessfully to get comfortable with the notion that we might have just shared a moment.

"Do you know Faustino?" he asked.

"Huh?"

"Faustino. You know, Bud Bundy. I thought you might know him."

"Why would you think I'd know Faustino?"

"Well fuck, man, you like *Married . . . with Children*, doncha?" came his fiery retort, as if that nebulous connection made perfect sense.

"I like Guns & Roses, too, but I don't know Slash!"

"You wanna meet him?" he asked.

"Who? Slash or Faustino?"

Bottomfeeder's face reddened. "For chrissakes, man, screw your head on straight! What the hell would you want to meet Faustino for? The guy can't act to save his life!"

Before I had a chance to answer, Bottomfeeder launched into a heated one-man debate over the likelihood of ever needing to deliver a great performance in order to stave off the Grim Reaper. On television a talking head was babbling about the push for campaign finance reform, and I tried to ascertain whether the stench in the air was emanating from stale ideas or my besotted roommate. Mostly, I couldn't help wondering how awesome it'd be to meet Slash. I bet that would be an especially interesting experience. So I called Fisher and asked him to try to arrange a meeting. He said he'd do his best, but in light of his disappointment over what had transpired at MTV, I wasn't really counting on it.

Step 7

A Woman of Some Importance

There was a knock on my door. It sounded like any other knock, say, from a FedEx guy or a neighbor wanting to borrow some sugar. But as I was about to discover, the person responsible for this knock that occurred on Super Bowl Sunday 2007 at 12:27 PM was no ordinary visitor. It was a knock from the Other Side.

"Who in a rat's ass could that be?" Bottomfeeder screamed from the kitchen.

"I don't know," I yelled back from the bathroom. "Why don't you answer it and find out?"

"Cuz I'm making the deviled eggs!"

I imagine everyone has peculiar traditions, and my freeloading roommate is no exception. In celebration of sporting events—including, but not limited to, the Super Bowl, World Series, NBA Finals, Stanley Cup, Masters, Bass Fishing Cup, NCAA Cheerleading Finals, Ultimate Fighting World Title, Great Wyoming Lumberjack Throw-Down, The Battle of the Network Stars, and the Pro Bowling

Seniors Championship—Bottomfeeder spends countless hours preparing deviled eggs from a secret recipe passed down through generations of freeloaders. Again, you've got *your* traditions, he's got his.

"Well, I'm on the toilet," I yelled back. "You'll *have* to get the door!"

From the kitchen came the sounds of loud grumbling along with some exaggerated rattling of pots and pans—B.F.'s way of letting me, and the unexpected visitor, know he was none too pleased with being disturbed while bedeviling. It couldn't be helped. I'd been on the porcelain throne for nearly an hour, stopped up worse than a hair clog in Donald Trump's sink. And at the rate things were going, I'd be damn lucky to be off the john by kickoff or even by the end of the first quarter, when we all believed the Super Bowl would be over, and the only important matter left to be settled would be the debate over which commercial ruled the most.

"It's for you," he said, and I recall that his voice seemed eerily *ill-omened*. "Somebody named Sylvia."

The most accurate way to convey what I felt next is this: imagine being struck by a lightning bolt. A lightning bolt made of ex-lax. Good-bye constipation, hello Worst Nightmare! Sylvia? SYLVIA?! I tried to convince myself that it couldn't be *that* Sylvia, yet sensing somehow that it most certainly was, panic set in. *Aspen* Sylvia? At my door? In California? I experienced a cacophonous ringing in my ears. Looking back, I would have preferred to have heard the shrill yelps of the Hounds of Hell.

How the . . . ? What the . . . ? Who the . . . ?

"He's right in there," I thought I heard Bottomfeeder saying. "Go ahead in."

I tried to scream no, but my voice failed me. And then she was standing there, right in front of me, and all I could say was, "I just crapped" . . . certainly not what I had dreamed I'd say if I were ever to see her again after lo these many lonely years. But "I just crapped" was all I could muster under such duress. And truth be told, it pretty much covered the bill.

"I'm back!" Sylvia gushed. "Did you miss me?"

I was never sure if being in love with Sylvia was exactly like having a sore tooth or owning a vintage Jaguar. The tooth argument: clamp down the jaw to see if it . . . OUCH! . . . still hurts. Push hard with the tongue to see if it . . . OH GOD! . . . still hurts. Forget all about her and sit down to a nice lunch and OH MY GOD IT STILL HURTS! Or, the Jag argument: you know you can't afford the maintenance she needs, but she sure looks amazing there beside the road as you leave to seek help. And here was Sylvia, big as life, setting my tongue twitching in reflex.

"You look great!" she said, which I found hard to believe. After all, I was sitting on the toilet with my pants around my ankles, wearing a pained expression that I imagine was not unlike the one Anne Frank must have sported when she first heard the knock on the attic door.

"Are you going to say something?" she asked.

You mean, *other* than the "I just crapped" thing? Probably not.

Then someone said, "Try one of these deviled eggs." Wait, did *I* say that? My mind plays tricks when I'm in cardiac arrest. No, it was Bottomfeeder, standing in the bathroom with Sylvia and me proffering a tray full of malodorous hors d'oeuvres. I believe this is exactly how Dante envisioned the Ninth Circle of Hell.

"Did you ever notice," B.F. said to Sylvia, "that on an emotional level, Jerry Springer guests tend to carry around more baggage than Paris Hilton on safari? Also, in every guest there seems to be a direct correlation among level of insanity, caloric intake, and the number of teeth missing."

Sylvia agreed, then swallowed a deviled egg whole.

"I'm Sylvia," she said to him, extending a hand. "Dan's girlfriend."

"I'm Bottomfeeder," he replied. "Dan's best friend."

Things I Never Wanted To Hear were suddenly slam-dancing in my cranial mosh pit. My *girlfriend?* My *best friend?* It was as though I'd shit myself into a horrific nightmare, filled with grotesque Maurice Sendak–esque creatures trying to pass themselves off as loved ones. There was only one thing to do. I got up off the toilet, steeled myself, looked Sylvia and B.F. square in the eyes, and said, "Do you wanna go to a bar and watch the game?"

◆ ♀ 🏆 ♀ ◆

It was in Aspen in the mid-'90s, around the time I started hanging out with Hunter S. Thompson (whoops, dropped something), that I met Sylvia and—to filch from yet another scribe—for me those were undoubtedly the best of times, and the worst of times. In a dizzying three-month span, I'd met and befriended both my literary hero and the woman of my dreams. Both relationships would bring me profound joy . . . and the two together would eventually shatter my brittle psyche like a dwarf tossed through a plate-glass window, except without the redeeming cuteness quotient that comes with the dwarf toss.

Ever since I left Aspen, I've gone to great lengths to purge the pain. I tried therapy, yoga, Tony Robbins tapes . . . I even dabbled with self-medication, or, as my probation officer referred to it, "a serious parole violation." And progress was made, friends. PROGRESS WAS MADE! Hell, up until that fateful knock on the door, I thought I was "pretty much over it"—which is safer than claiming to be "completely over it," because then you'd *know* I'm entirely full of shit. So, yeah, I was doing good, all right, and then someone chucked the Dwarf of Heartache through the glass again. And if you're wondering whodunit, well, allow me to give you a hint. . . .

"So," Sylvia said, trying to break seven years' worth of ice at O'Brien's pub while I attempted to quell my exquisite inner pain with copious amounts of a concoction called a Plank Walker,*"I read in the paper that some screenwriter was just paid lots of money to adapt one of Hunter Thompson's books into a movie. . . . Weren't you gonna do that? You know, before you two had that fight?"

I nodded numbly, then gestured for the bartender—my Plank Walker needed a bit more **Chartreuse**. As he topped off the cocktail I wondered if professional chefs sweat the small beer like I do when they go out to eat. For instance, if Mario Batali were dining at Bobby Flay's restaurant in Manhattan, would he send back a lobster–toasted garlic quesadilla with brie cheese if the dish were a tad light on tarragon relish? Or would that just make Mario look like a dick?

---

* Good for what ails anyone suffering from severe heartache: 1 1/2 oz. Johnnie Walker Red Scotch whisky, a 1/2 oz. Rosso vermouth, and a 1/2 oz. Yellow Chartreuse. Stir the ingredients into a rocks glass three-quarters filled with ice.

❧ In Search of . . . Chartreuse ❧

Folklore, of the sort propagated by resourceful publicists, has it that the recipe for the liqueur Chartreuse is a mystery to the entire world excepting three Carthusian monks cloistered inside a monastery in the French Alps. And even those three holy men each knows but a portion of the complete formula. Protecting trade secrets is one thing, but this sounds a bit excessive if you ask me. After all, if you can't trust a cloistered monk, then who in the hell can you trust? (Oprah, maybe? The Dalai Lama?) What we do know about the production of the mysterious Chartreuse is that it contains more than 130 herbs and botanicals, it's the only liqueur to be aged in oak vats, and the Carthusian Order has been at it nonstop for four hundred years.

There are two types of Chartreuse: green and yellow. The former is intensely floral, with strong hints of fennel, rosemary, cinnamon, and cloves. Yellow Chartreuse is the more citrusy of the two, brimming with flavors such as blood orange, lemon, and honey. Chartreuse isn't really the type of elixir to be enjoyed straight, but it can really spruce up a cocktail. Fortunately, I know a guy on the inside at the monastery who managed to smuggle out a few cocktail recipes:

continued on next page >>

"That would have been great—all that money. If, you know, you two hadn't had that fight. Plus, Johnny Depp and Josh Hartnett have signed on to star in it. It's going to be huge."

I suppressed the urge to vomit.

"A couple of years before he died," Bottomfeeder interjected, "Thompson left a couple of crazed messages on the machine, threatening to sue Dan . . . or shoot him . . . or maybe both. Something to do with selling out to the Man."

Sylvia produced a newspaper clipping from her purse. "Yep," she said, reading, "the writer got a couple hundred grand to adapt that book."

"Dan pissed Hunter off because he has some rich Republican

Mona's Smile

by Janice Brown

0.5 oz. Green Chartreuse

0.5 oz. Calvados (apple brandy)

1.61803 oz. rye or bourbon blended whiskey

3–4 hearty dashes of Amaro Ramazzotti Liqueur water (club soda optional)

Shake all the ingredients in a cocktail shaker half-filled with ice. Strain into a chilled cocktail glass and garnish with a pyramid-shaped Jerusalem artichoke cube and a cherry on a sword pick.

Chartreuse Fizz

as featured at Diner in Brooklyn, NY

1 oz. gin

0.75 oz. Green Chartreuse

0.5 oz. lime juice

Fill with soda on the rocks in a Collins glass.

friends, and cuz he drops Hunter's name everywhere," Bottomfeeder continued. "Wait . . . did you just say a couple hundred grand?"

"Yep."

"Wow."

"Damn."

At that I did vomit.

⋅ 🍸 🍸 🍸 ⋅

"Now might not be the best time for this," Sylvia said as she wiped the puke from my chin in the alley behind the bar, "but the reason I came back after all these years is that I've got something to tell you. . . ."

You know that moment in a horror movie when the eerie music kicks in? Right before someone gets his head hacked off by a guy in a hockey mask or something nasty like that? Well . . .

EXT. ALLEY BEHIND BAR—NIGHT

Sylvia, wiping the vomit from Dan's chin, is about to tell him something. She puts on a hockey mask.

CUE EERIE MUSIC.

SYLVIA: I'm getting married, Dan . . . to Tommy . . . you know, your
      former best friend.

SFX: An ominous sting. Dan bites his lower lip completely off.

SYLVIA: I know this might be a bit of a shocker, but believe me,
      Tommy and I want nothing more than for you to be okay with
      this. In fact, we very much want to have your blessing. Which is
      why Tommy would like you . . .

Dan—lower-lipless, bleeding, and covered in his own waste—tries to throw himself under a PASSING BUS. He misses, and lands in a puddle of MOTOR OIL. Sylvia continues assaulting him with RAZOR-SHARP VERBAL DAGGERS.

SYLVIA (cont'd): . . . to be his best man.

Dan inexplicably begins laughing. Only it doesn't sound much like laughter because of the MISSING LOWER LIP AND THE BLOOD AND THE MOTOR OIL.

Sylvia is perplexed.

SYLVIA: Are . . . are you okay?

More hysterical laughter.

SYLVIA: Dan?

Laugh, laugh, laugh! Blood and motor oil spewing everywhere.

SYLVIA: Honey, will you . . . will you be Tommy's best man?

Dan suddenly stops laughing, cocks his head, and eyes her suspiciously.

SYLVIA: Will you?

Dan reaches to the ground, picks up his lower lip, and miraculously reattaches it.

DAN: I'm gonna need some time . . . to think.

FADE OUT

⚲ 🍸 ⚲

"So she's getting married, and you're still single. Boo-fucking-hoo, brutha. Besides, what's wrong with being single?" Bottomfeeder asked me as I drowned some blues in **Southern Comfort** at O'Brien's. "I mean, you're good at it. *Really* good at it. I think it's the one thing that separates you from ordinary people." He had a point . . . and *that* certainly didn't make me feel any better about the situation. It's one thing to be lonely in this world; it's quite another to realize that, were you *not* alone, you'd be altogether less interesting.

❧ I'm So Hot for Her, but She's SoCo ❧

They say old habits die hard, but it says here that some old habits—particularly the unhealthy kind—occasionally die overnight. Such was the case with my Southern Comfort habit. The spiced whiskey-flavored liqueur bills itself as a "New Orleans original," though these days it's produced and bottled in Louisville, Kentucky. Roll back to the summer of 1995: I was dancing under the stars on the balcony of the Cat's Meow in the Big Easy's French Quarter, having just drained the last of what was undoubtedly not my first Southern Comfort Strawberry Frappé of the evening. And that's when it hit me . . . the ground. Or, I hit it, rather. Instantly swore off SoCo and the funky chicken forever.

Ten years later at a Mardi Gras–themed soiree in Hermosa Beach, Southern Comfort came calling again. Our hostess—and indeed she was the "mostest"—served up Southern Hurricanes that bore little resemblance to New Orleans's most celebrated libation. But that's not to say it wasn't dang tasty. So good, in fact, that I took a bottle of SoCo home with me that night—we cuddled and made up; even did a few steps from the funky chicken.

Southern Hurricane
1.5 oz Southern Comfort
splash of grenadine
lemon-lime soda

Fill Hurricane glass with ice. Add all ingredients and stir. Garnish with an orange wedge and a cherry.

"It's been five years!" I blurted. "Five years since that evil woman . . . no, never mind . . . I swore I'd never talk about it again."

But I couldn't help it. What she had done—the perfidy of it all!—made me a hard man, and not in the good way. Sylvia had yanked out my heart, thrown it on the floor, and performed a *Lord of the Dance* number all over it. By the time she was through, my spirit had been broken more than a two-bit club fighter's nose. I became a shell of the man I used to be, which, come to think of it, really wasn't all that much of a man to begin with. And I was haunted by my own improvidence. Sylvia and I had shared what is popularly known as an "open relationship." Ostensibly, an open relationship is one based on mutual respect for individuality and a belief in personal freedom. But all it *really* meant was that both of us were free to screw around on each other. Had I been the one who'd decided we should have an open relationship, everything would have been dandy. I wasn't, though, because I'm the old-fashioned type who figures if you really respect somebody in a relationship then you ought to have the decency to sneak around and keep your cheating to yourself.

"I think I'd like to keep things wide open," Sylvia had told me at the beginning of our doomed dalliance, and she made no real mention that "things" included those long legs of hers. And at first I was all for it. I figured I'd be able to indulge my primal male hunter-gatherer urges guilt-free, *and* still have a steady, attractive date lined up for Saturday nights. Men invented the concept of the open relationship for this very reason: to have our cake . . . and eat lots of other people's cakes, too! The problem was that I had quickly grown to love the cake I had with Sylvia. A few weeks into our arrange-ment, I started wondering—obsessing over, actually—who, besides me, might be sampling her icing. All at once, Jealousy, Insecurity, and Lame Metaphors began rearing their ugly heads. And so it was that I made my way into a crowded bar one night to calm my nerves with Strong Drink, and noticed a cute couple snuggling in a booth across the way. That's when I discovered the excruciating downside of the open relationship.

"Sylvia, what in the name of Jack fucking Daniels are you doing with my best friend?" I shrieked.

That was Tommy Barnard,* a pilot I had met when I was sta-tioned in **Venezuela** with the Merchant Marine.† Tommy and I had a lot of common interests, such as going out drinking, staying in drinking, and . . . well, assorted . . . other . . . things . . . like drinking. I'd tell you more about Tommy Barnard, but then I'd be breaking yet another vow—the one about never speaking his cursed name again—and I WILL stick to my vow never to break more than two vows in a single chapter.

ϟ Cha-Cha-Cha Cachaça! ϟ

At this writing, I'm reminded that America's reigning pulpit-pounding crackpot, Pat Robertson, recently upset many of the folks in Venezuela by suggesting in no uncertain terms that we send assassins down there to kill their president. Now, some might say that's just Pat being Pat—in the past the septuagenarian *700 Club* founder has, after all, compared left-leaning citizens of this country to Nazis; claimed that the feminist movement encourages women to kill their chil-dren, practice witchcraft, and become lesbians; and accused little Halloween trick-or-treaters of Satanism . . . and nobody here really seems to care all that much.

Venezuela's best-known export is Angostura Bitters, which doesn't lend itself to

continued on next page >>

---

* Not his real name, but it might as well have been.

† Not really, but it makes for a better story.

After Sylvia left with that backstabbing louche ex-friend who shall remain nameless, I launched into an aberrant mode of behavior: for the rest of the evening, when I wasn't pounding beers at the bar, I attempted to utilize those fabricated stories, pitiable pickup lines, and sultry facial expressions I had foolishly convinced myself amounted to personality, in the desperate hope that I'd meet someone else, too. It didn't happen. What did happen was that in a relatively short period of time I managed to make a raging ass of myself, ensuring that for the rest of the evening women avoided me like a second-string Junior Varsity defensive back with bad skin. Then, sometime around 2:00 AM, I burst into my apartment, picked up the phone, and called that person I thought was my girlfriend—determined to tell her how I *really* felt. She wasn't home. She was probably still foreplaying with Tom, er ... THAT GUY!

Uh-oh. In a night littered with poor decisions on my part, I made yet another dubious move. I left a message: "Where are you, Sylvia? Could you actually be spending the night with that asshole? That lamppost licker with the off-the-rack wardrobe and red Miata?

warm-weather cocktails, so allow me to instead suggest something from neighboring Brazil: cachaça (pronounced KUH-shah-suh), the rumlike spirit that is the key ingredient in the refreshing caipirinha. The name translates roughly to "farmer's drink," but the caipirinha has outgrown its bumpkin beginnings and become quite popular in trendy Big City establishments.

Made with lime, sugar, and two ounces of cachaça—Beliza Pura is an outstanding brand—the key to a great caipirinha is in the muddling. Place eight lime wedges pulp-side up in a glass and sprinkle with sugar. With a pestle, use mild pressure and a twisting motion to release the juice in the flesh, not crushing the skin, which is high in unwanted bitter oils. And as Pat Robertson would no doubt attest, the only thing worse than a bitter caipirinha is a pack of liberal lesbo devil-kids coming to your door begging for sweets.

Don't you realize what a hideous mistake you're making? Don't you know how much cooler I am than him? HOW COULD YOU DO THIS TO ME??!!" To add indignity to disaster, all of her girlfriends would get to listen to my psychobabble, as it was permanently saved on her answering machine. She would play it over and over again—inviting friends by to hear it, posting it on the Internet, and calling random social workers in places like Ohio who made poor second-generation tapes to play on their way to work at the Volunteer Center. In one disastrous evening, I'd lost my girl, my best bud, and my dignity. Had it not been for my ol' pal beer, well, I don't know what I would have remembered. Then I moved to California to start over.

"Here's what I think, Dan," Bottomfeeder offered. "A relationship is like the inside of a jar of paste. Even with the lid securely fastened, it's sticky and hard to handle. Leave it open, and it'll quickly harden and become useless."

Bottomfeeder was right, of course. (Twice in one day—no doubt a record that may never be broken.) I wanted to tell him more about Sylvia and me. I wanted to tell him that despite her cheatin' ways, she was the most intriguing woman I'd ever met. I wanted to tell him about the way she walked. And the way she wore her hair. And, well, about the sweet, sweet love we had made.

"Hey, man," I said, tossing an arm around his shoulder. "Let's play darts."

Some things are better left unsaid.

＋♈ 🏆 ♈＋

In my nonage, I did the majority of my underage drinking in the dark alleys and on the dirty street corners of Philadelphia. As I got older—you know, sixteen or so—the party moved from the street to the local VFW Hall, where on any given weekend night hundreds of rowdy neighborhood teens would drink themselves oblivious at a festivity known as a Beef & Beer.

Now, for those of you who have never experienced a Beef & Beer—and I'm assuming that to be pretty much everyone who *didn't* grow up in Philly, because, like cheesesteaks and communities comprised entirely of extraordinarily obese people, it's a regional phenomenon—all you really need to know is that B&Bs were good, clean fun. We drank a lot, fought a little, and on the good nights got to play tonsil hockey with a big-haired cheerleader or two. The cops left us alone because damn near every kid in the neighborhood was related to a cop, and because the guys who ran the B&Bs invariably left a "spare" keg outside for the boys in blue to enjoy down at the station.

They don't do Beef & Beers in L.A. I'm sure they never have. And it's a safe bet that the teenagers in Philly don't have 'em anymore, either, but since I'm in L.A. now, and an adult (or so my ID says), and this story is about something that happened four years ago, well . . . Christ, am I off on a tangent here or what?

My point is this: four years ago, raves were all the rage with kids. I don't know why these parties were called that, because from what I witnessed at the one and only rave I've ever been to, nobody seemed to be talking with any real enthusiasm. In fact, nobody was talking much at all; they were too dazed, and *definitely* too confused. If you ask me, instead of "raves" they should have called 'em "Ecstasy & Evians," as that's what every pimply-faced kid I encountered seemed to be ingesting.

"Isn't this great?" Sylvia yelled. Or maybe she said, "I'm in first grade." The DJ—who called himself Logic Bomb—had the music amped up to such earsplitting levels that he made the soundman for the Who look like a freakin' pussy.

"Maybe you should go talk to Tommy," she screamed. "I think he's upset."

Sylvia, in her dementia—and that is the fairest term I could find to describe the woman's thought processes—had decided to "reunite" me with my former best friend Tommy, her then-fiancé, at a rave. She thought it would be a "super cool and relaxing" place for us to hash out our differences—the first and foremost being that I wanted, more than anything, for Tommy to be dead.

"Don't you think he looks upset?" she hollered, gesturing toward Tommy, who was bobbing his head numbly, utterly rapt by the condensation on his Evian bottle.

"He's not upset," I howled above the din, "he's on E!"

"*Ornery?* What makes you think he's ornery?" she shrieked.

"He's not ornery . . . he's *on E!*"

"Well, of course he's lonely. You're ignoring him!"

"Sylvia"—and I was now bellowing in her ear—"I can't do this!"

"I know you're *cartoonish* . . . that's what I always loved about you! That's what Tommy always loved about you. Look at him over there; he's a mess without you."

Tommy was rolling around on the floor, wrestling with what appeared to be a large glow stick.

"You *are* going to be his best man, aren't you, Dan?"

I was about to tell her I'd rather dip my freshly shaved ass in jalapeño sauce.

"It'll be fun . . . and you'll get to plan his bachelor party."

"Look, Sylvia," I screamed, "I'm flattered and all, but I just can't . . . wait, did you just say I get to plan his bachelor party? Or was it 'Hugo owns a spatula named Artie?'"

Sylvia looked at me as though I were crazy. And suddenly I was: crazy with ideas about how to make Tommy's bachelor party a night NONE of us would ever forget. Hell, I knew hookers—still do— most of whom have several nasty diseases. And I know of sex clubs in seedy neighborhoods. The kind of places where a bachelor might go for his last piece of premarital ass, and leave wrapped in trash bags in the trunk of some gangbanger's hoopty.

As Best Man and Master of Bachelor Party Ceremonies, I would be in complete control of my ol' pal Tommy for one glorious night that would certainly spell the end of his and Sylvia's unholy union. Ahh . . . Revenge . . . what a sweet, seductive mistress you appear!

. ♀ ♈ ♀ .

"You sure this place is safe, dude?" Tommy asked nervously as we made our way to the secret back room at Chuck Shmitt's Knuckle Lounge and Strip-A-Torium.* "A lot of these people look like they should be in prison."

* It's since been shut down and replaced by Starbucks . . . two of them.

It was just like Tommy to be afraid of a few hookers and recently paroled hit men. From the moment I met the guy in Kent's Pub* outside of London, I knew he was what the British refer to as a "poofter." Hell, even Darby, the heavily tattooed and pierced barkeep at Kent's, agreed with me. And if the wimpy Brits think you're soft, you've got a Valium's chance in Anna Nicole Smith's late medicine cabinet of surviving the secret back room at Chuck Shmitt's Knuckle Lounge and Strip-A-Torium in El Segundo.

Hell, if it hadn't been for me and my AK-47, Tommy the Poofter would never even have made it out of that Venezuelan brothel,† and it's for damn sure he never would have gotten an honorable discharge from the Merchant Marine. But hell, those are other stories for other times. Especially with Glenda the Dirty Ho scheduled to arrive in just a few short minutes.

A few short minutes later . . .

It's one thing to have others refer to you as a Dirty Ho; it's quite another to introduce yourself thusly. And then it's another thing altogether to have the unsavory moniker stitched on the lapel of your motorcycle-gang jacket.

"Tommy, I'd like you to meet—"

"Glenda the Dirty Ho?" He seemed a bit, um, surprised.

"So you can read—congratulations!" Glenda spat as Tommy stared incredulously at the dangerously chaotic voluptuousness that forms the most infamous call girl in all of Southern California. "But can you work the thrill drill, Sparky?"

---

* also now a Starbucks

† recently converted to a Coffee Bean & Tea Leaf

Then, before he could utter a word, she dragged him into the back room.

"Have fun, Tommy!" I yelled after them. "She's my bachelor party present to you!"

I figured there was no point in mentioning that I'd paid Glenda the Dirty Ho to kill my former best friend Tommy; he'd find out in a few moments.

A few moments later . . .

Glenda the Dirty Ho emerged from the back room, covered in sweat and breathing heavily. Despite his poofterity, Tommy must have been a tough kill.

"Whatcha do with the body, Glenda?"

"Well, first I put his cock in my mouth—"

"Wait, wait, wait. . . . You didn't have to screw him before you killed 'im. I'm not paying extra for that!"

"I didn't kill him," Glenda said in a gentle, womanly tone I'd never imagined I'd hear coming from the harsh likes of a grizzled biker ho. "We fell in love. He's out back on my Harley waitin' for me. He wanted me to tell you thanks, and good-bye."

And I didn't know whether to shit or go blind . . . so I did both . . . or at least it felt as though I did. Then I called Bottomfeeder and told him I needed him at Chuck Shmitt's, pronto.

· ♀ ♈ ♀ ·

"I think the J. Geils Band really nailed it when they sang 'Love Stinks.' Man, ain't that the truth?" Bottomfeeder mumbled through a mouthful of pretzels and beer. Yeah, and ain't that the first J. Geils Band reference I've heard in, oh, about fifteen years?* And hey, barkeep, could you pour me another shot of Jim Beam, please?

"Here's what I think you should do when Sylvia gets here . . ." Bottomfeeder continued.

Oh, boy! Just what I'd been hoping for.

"You see, Dan," my alleged best friend went on, "there are all kinds of farters in the world. There are the honest ones that admit they farted, but offer good medical reasons; the dishonest kind that fart and then blame the dog; and then there are the strategic farters who conceal their farts with loud coughing. Finally, there are the unfortunate ones who try awfully hard to fart but crap themselves instead. . . . You see what I'm getting at?"

"No! No! No! No! No! No! WHAT IN THE HELL ARE YOU GETTING AT, MAN?!!" If there's a more cryptic individual in the universe, I haven't met him or her.

"What I'm getting at is, if you're a dishonest farter, you're gonna get caught in a stinkin' lie," Bottomfeeder said coolly. "This whole business with Tommy and Glenda the Dirty Ho is like a nasty fart: it stinks. But you gotta tell Sylvia the truth, no matter how bad it is."

---

* The J. Geils Band, which broke up in 1985, scored a massive hit with "Centerfold" in 1981. The track's risqué video proved a revelation to an entire generation of horny teenaged boys, me among them, who for the very first time realized the full masturbatory possibilities of MTV. Madonna came along shortly thereafter and nearly killed us all.

And somehow, some way, that malodorous riddle of Bottom-feeder's made perfect sense.

Four hours later . . .

"Sometimes I think it would be great to be a man," Sylvia slurred, her lips numbed by one too many pain-killing Sloe Gin Fizzes. "You can open all your own jars, people never stare at your chest when you're talking to them, wrinkles add character, the same hairstyle lasts for years, maybe decades, and best of all you can silently watch a game with a buddy for hours without thinking, *He must be mad at me.*"

"Um, Sylvia, are . . . are you okay?" I asked apprehensively.

"You mean besides the fact that my fiancé just ran off with something called Bimbo the Stinking Slut. . . ."

"Glenda the Dirty Ho," I corrected her.

"Yeah, whatever . . . well, besides that I guess I'm . . . I'm . . . WAAAAAAAAHHHHHHH!!!!!!"

I hugged her tightly, muffling her ululations. Not out of concern, necessarily—I was, after all, reveling in her pain—it was just that any loud noise at Chuck Shmitt's usually led to trouble.

"Ohhhh, I hate that Tommy," Sylvia wailed. "He's such a . . . a . . . piece of . . . foreskin!"

Foreskin? Well, I had to admit that was a new one.

"You ever wonder what happens to the foreskin after a circumcision?" Bottomfeeder mused. "Do they just throw it away?"

I had myself always figured how cool it would be if, like, they kept it for later. You know, so someday when the guys were sitting around drinking beers, playing poker, and comparing battle scars a guy would be like, "Yeah, so I got this scar on my leg playing rugby in college."

Then another guy would go, "That's nothing; I busted all ten of my fingers at an underground fight club." Finally, another one would whip out his foreskin, slap it on the table, and say, "Back off, chumps! When I was a baby some dude lopped off half my schwantz . . . and I barely cried."

Instead, I said, "Jesus, man! Show a little sensitivity! Poor Sylvia here just had to call off her wedding, for chrissakes!" And then I had to fight hard to suppress a grin.

It was done. The wedding was off. Tommy was gone. Sylvia was back. And I was . . . I was . . . oh . . . no . . .

I WAS STUCK WITH HER—AGAIN!!!!!

Step 8

Chick Drinks and the Men Who Drink Them

The woman in the apartment directly across from mine has a thirteen-year-old daughter, and most days after school the girl and several of her friends gather to do what newly teenaged girls like to do most: yak. And squeal. And shriek. And make noises akin to what I imagine it would sound like if Michael Jackson were to be violated by a mule.* And these girls do this at decibel levels that make roaring jet engines seem like white noise. Alan Jay Lerner and Frederick Loewe—the guys who wrote "Thank Heaven for Little Girls"†—weren't living next to one while they were penning that saccharine ditty, because if they had been, I can assure you they'd have changed their tune. "Thank Heaven for Birth Control," perhaps?

---

* high-pitched "hee-hees" intermixed with lusty "hee-haws"

† The guy who sang it, Maurice Chevalier, was from France, where grown men have been known to drink like little girls. One of the more dainty concoctions I've come across in my research in Paris is the Malabar Shooter, offered exclusively at a little bar called L'Artscenik near the Moulin Rouge. Bar owner Stephane Lesc's creation calls for bubble gum (Malabar is France's version of Bazooka) soaked in a bottle of Saint James Caribbean Rum mixed with 1/4 cup of sugar. The resulting shot is like candy for grown-ups. You can use any rum you like, actually, but be sure to allow the gum to macerate for at least twenty-four hours.

Don't get me wrong—I like teenage girls, if only because they're so close to growing up into **women**. And I love women at least as passionately as L.A. cops hate camcorders. But until they're of legal age, well, frankly I just don't have much use for them. And when I'm on deadline and the teenyboppers are in full screech, well, they can just kiss mah grits!

⚡ Three for the Ladies ⚡

Here are a few libations aimed at those on the distaff side who have—thank heaven—attained womanhood:

Barbie Shot

Sure, it sounds like an out-and-out chick drink, but men dig 'em plenty.

1 oz. Malibu rum
1 oz. vodka
1 oz. cranberry juice
1 oz. orange juice

Combine all ingredients in an ice-filled shaker. Shake, chill, and strain it into a cocktail glass.

Absolut Sex

The name isn't the only alluring thing about this one.

1 oz. Absolut Kurant
1 oz. Midori melon liqueur
1 oz. cranberry juice

Same serving procedure as above, with a splash of lemon-lime soda added on top.

The Startini

A major meteor shower passed through our solar system a while back, and wouldn't you know that the folks at Moët Hennessy came up with a few champagne cocktails to toast

continued on next page >>

the bright lights in the sky. You gotta hand it to the promotions people in the wine and spirits industry, who seem to have a limitless capacity to exploit special (and not so special) events in order to sell more hootch. Christmas, Easter, Kwanzaa, the season premiere of *Dancing with the Stars* . . . just name the occasion, and there have likely been scores of cleverly named cocktails created to celebrate it. Having a Super Bowl party? Break out the Hail Mary Margaritas! They're drafting a constitution in Iraq? Try a Baghdad Bomber or a delicious Fallujah Fizz! It's that time of the month again, eh? Well . . . you get the picture.

0.5 oz. vodka
lemon sorbet
Moët Nectar Impérial

Add a spoonful of sorbet to a martini glass and stir in the vodka. Fill the glass with the champagne.

For instance, I'd intended this section to elucidate the memory-enhancing powers of sage and its usefulness in combating the effects of Mind Erasers,* but the cacophonic cabal next door has been running sonic interference for going on two hours now, and I find myself getting sucked into their myriad meaningless debates . . . which seem to be raging all at once: Who's hotter—Zac Efron or Dylan Sprouse? Is Miley Cyrus for real, and does she have the staying power of Ashlee Simpson? Which Olsen twin is cooler? And—my favorite—does smoking make your boobs bigger?

These are the issues that challenge young girls in these troubled times, and quite frankly, I'm very alarmed by the trend. After all, any

---

* Mind Erasers are wussy shots consisting of equal parts vodka, Kahlúa, and tonic water.

idiot knows that Zac is waaaaay cutest, and that Miley has more talent in her push-up bra than Ashlee has in her whole body. As for the Olsens, they're, like, totally 2005. And smoking doesn't enhance the chest, girls, but it will make the boys think you're easy, so fire up those Camel Lights.

As I finished that last sentence, I heard one of the girls complain about the "gruel" served in her school cafeteria. Now, I don't imagine she meant it literally, but her remark did get me to thinking: I bet gruel wouldn't be all that bad if it simply weren't called "gruel." What if it were called "sugar-yummy" instead? Can't imagine you'd hear many people complain about getting a bowl of "sugar-yummy," no matter how shitty it tasted. If I were over in my neighbor's condo hanging with the girls right now, I'd raise this point—perhaps even suggest we start a campaign down at the middle school to have gruel officially renamed. Not that they'd care, because in the time it took me to preserve the thought, the girls had already moved on to a more pressing matter: should they go to the mall, or stay in and paint their nails?

"Mall!" I screamed, like I'd suddenly come down with Tourrette's Syndrome.

Then there was dead silence . . . followed by a complete hush, and finally, no sound whatsoever.

"Who was that?" one of them eventually whispered, loud enough for me to hear.

"I think it's my creepy neighbor," the girl next door replied. "He's into botany."

At this, they sniggered en masse.

"How *old* is he?" another one hissed.

"OLD! Like, he listens to Guns & Roses and plays golf and wears clogs and stuff!"

More sniggering, along with a smattering of titters.

I was beside myself, because Tiger Woods plays golf and nobody accuses him of being a **geezer**. As for the clogs, well, that's complete bunk—I don't wear clogs! They're authentic Dutch wooden shoes that my friend Gijsbert shipped over from Rotterdam. And I only wear them on Sundays when I go to the market to buy sage, and . . . and . . . and Guns & Roses rocks and . . . who are they calling *old*? I'm

---

⚡ We Thank You for Your Support Bra ⚡

While we're on the subject of getting old, it's hard to believe it's been twenty-two years since Bartles & Jaymes Premium Wine Coolers first hit the shelves. Fueled by a popular TV ad campaign featuring two countrified old gents who were mighty dang appreciative of the drinking public's support, B&J quickly became the world's number-one-selling brand. Then, almost as quickly, people stopped buying wine coolers, and Ed (the quiet one) and Frank (the guy who did the thanking) went the way of Lionel Richie chart-toppers, Jordache jeans, and Pac-Man.

But like my senile grandmother, history tends to repeat itself, and in recent years Bartles & Jaymes has made a bit of a comeback. Truth is, their coolers are pretty damn tasty and not nearly as emasculating a retro-malt-beverage as, say, Zima. The stuff's cheap, too, and comes in twelve cocktail-inspired flavors, including such '80s staples as the Fuzzy Navel and Piña Colada. What, no Alabama Slammer?

---

as spry as, well, as anyone can be who actually uses words like "spry."

"You kids better keep it down over there or I'll call the cops!" I found myself shouting out the window while simultaneously bemoaning my inability to recall the lyrics to "Sweet Child O' Mine." Clearly, I'm not getting enough sage in my diet.

"And I'm not *old*, girls," I continued, "I just don't like noise when I've got work to do and bills to pay and my back is aching—and is it 'She's got eyes of the bluest skies' or 'eyes of the blues guys'? Boy, has it really been *eighteen years* since that song was released? Seems like yesterday."

The girls, incidentally, had already left for the mall, where they would no doubt be yapping loudly about things such as Daniel Radcliffe's cuddliness factor. Too bad I couldn't join them. It was for the best anyway, cuz what did they know? Old? *Me?* Old, my ass! I was just a little out of sorts because I still had deadlines hanging over me. I figured I'd better fix myself a glass of warm milk, soak my feet, and watch some *Murder She Wrote*. That'd make me feel better.

Then again, maybe those girls were on to something.... You see, just last week I pulled a muscle in my back. The injury itself was distressing enough, as my threshold for pain is lower than the IQ of most blonde porn stars. The thing is, it wasn't the nagging pain in my lower back that troubled me the most, it was *how* it got there. It was *how* I hurt myself.

I did it yawning.

On the way home from my weekly Mon-Khmer lesson* I had occasion to stop and reflect upon life, and in that moment of quiet reverie I involuntarily opened my mouth wide and breathed in deeply . . . and that's when something suddenly "popped" slightly to the north of my butt crack.

When I was a young man—say, thirty-five—I had a swaggering

---

* I've got a real passion for Austroasiatic languages.

aura about me underscored by a sense of invincibility. I could run fast, jump high, party hard, and make love like a porn star (insert your own IQ zinger here). When you're a young man, the world is your raw oyster, and it's just waiting for you to slurp it down whole, with a cold beer chaser. When you're a young man, you feel as indomitable as a Roger Clemens fastball. And then one day, the simple act of yawning becomes too much for your body to handle. That's the day you cease to be a young man ingesting bivalve mollusks to put the carnal ocean in motion. That's the day you're reduced to tossing weak, Charlie Hough–like knucklers. That's the day you first notice the shadow of a Social Security check creeping across the lawn. That day, you get old. Floored by this realization, I did what everybody in Hollywood does in the midst of a personal crisis: I called my agent.

"I'M OLD!" I howled. "I just hurt myself yawning!"

"Have you told anyone else yet?" my agent replied, his voice tinged with panic.

"Uh . . . no . . . why?"

He breathed an audible sigh of relief. "Whatever you do, DON'T LET ANYONE KNOW YOU'RE OLD!" he shouted. "In this business, you get old, you die."

I blanched, then did what everybody in Hollywood does when an agent starts dispensing specious counsel: I hung up and went to **Starbucks.***

---

* There was a time in my life when I harbored a deep resentment for the coffee giant (see sidebar on the next page), but I did a volte-face and today proudly count myself among the company's most loyal customers.

ϟ An Open Letter to Howard Schultz, Chairman and Chief Global Strategist, Starbucks ϟ

(The following note was composed several years ago, prior to my Starbucks conversion.)

Dear Howard:

I'd ask how you're doing, but I think we both know the answer to that already, don't we? Damn, dawg, 6,500 Starbucks stores worldwide, and counting. That's a helluva lot of caramel macchiatos, isn't it? I mean, seriously, we've got, like, two or three hundred of the goddamn places here in Santa Monica alone. Oops, sorry . . . I cussed. You'll have to forgive me, it's just that . . . well, Howie, it's just that I've got a bit of a bone to pick with Starbucks. Actually, that's not entirely accurate. Truth is, I FUCKING HATE STARBUCKS!!!

There, I said it. I FUCKING HATE STARBUCKS! Again, Howie, I apologize for the off-color language, because I realize you may very well be an upstanding guy with strong family values, ties to all the right charities, and the whole bag of worms. But it feels SO GOOD to finally share my feelings with you. No kidding, man, I hold Starbucks in the same esteem as pop-up Internet ads, telemarketers, and aggressive meter maids. Given a choice between a lifetime supply of Starbucks coffee and a wicked case of West Nile Virus, I say, "Bring on the mosquitos."

Now, you're probably thinking that my lack of Pure Love for Starbucks comes down to some lefty political leanings or heartfelt concerns about mom-and-pop coffeehouses going the way of Britney Spears's career. But you're wrong. I don't give a flying frappuccino if your beans come from shade-grown, fair-trade fields where they're picked exclusively by virgins under a full moon. Nor do I give a damn if you drive every washed-up hippie out of the mild-but-legal stimulant game and back into

continued on next page >>

How did I get so soft? I wondered while sipping a frothy triple caramel macchiato. It seemed like only yesterday that I was strong and virile. I'd spent a lifetime doing things a hell of a lot more strenuous than yawning, and not once had I ever come up lame. It dawned on me that I needed to get in shape. I figured the best way to do so was to resume my cardiovascular routine. The problem was that I couldn't

University Studies where they belong. No, my friend, I hate Starbucks because of your customers.

Especially those with unmonitored car alarms who park under my window every morning. That's right—I live next to one of your Starbucks (and at the current rate of expansion, one of every three buildings in the Developed World will be a Starbucks in about 22.3 years, give or take a week). What the hell do these people need with a keyless entry that blows the horn when they lock the door? Is their Volvo-separation anxiety so great they need that reassurance? Is it because the car can't actually wave good-bye as they head into the damn caffeine den? And, judging by the lot below my window, it is YOUR CUSTOMERS who are responsible for the continued existence of the Swedish auto industry. How do you live with that on your conscience?

Yes, I know them well, those decaf-swilling early risers who apparently don't understand that some mornings "quiet time" needs to extend into the early afternoon. It's been years since they have been out until 4:30 AM quaffing adult beverages and then suffering through the intensity of superhuman-hearing hangovers—those hangovers that amplify the sound of their damn alarms to the point where it's like being inside the amps at a Gwar concert.

So there you have it. Get rid of the customers and we've got no problem. Hell, some of my best friends are suppliers of stimulants! But my guess is that you won't budge on that one, Howie. So I'm gonna sit here and train pigeons to shit on the hoods of those shiny mommy-mobiles, and I'm gonna stick pins into a voodoo doll crafted from those wraparound heat shields that keep those tender fingers from touching the cup. My printer is cranking out "Free Starbucks Coffee" fliers that I'm gonna hand out to homeless people this afternoon, and then I'll stop by a real diner for some non-designer java. Thanks for your time, and for indulging this cathartic rant, which for me turned out to be good to the very last drop.

quite remember what that routine entailed. Then I remembered: I never *had* a cardiovascular routine. Caffeine and cigarettes kept me thin in college.

Perhaps it was too late, anyway. When yawns precipitate back spasms, it augurs an impending respite on a mortician's slab. Surely my postmortem corporeal decomposition cycle had gotten off to an early start. At any moment, a sneeze could cause my spleen to rupture. One bad case of the hiccups and I'm done for. In the end, I decided I wasn't getting enough Starbucks products in my diet. Caffeine, after all, is a stimulant that wards off yawning. In fact, sipping my second frothy triple caramel macchiato of the day, I began to feel like a million bucks again. So I did what everybody in Hollywood does when they're thinking millions: I started writing a screenplay. Tentatively titled *The Old Man and the Sea of Hip-Hoppers*, my script chronicles the adventures of a feeble thirtysomething scribe who reconnects with his youth by getting tattooed and pierced beyond recognition. My agent loves the concept—he thinks we can get Tracy Nelson to sign on to play the female lead.

And I've gotten serious about reversing the process of my deteriorating physical condition. Fisher hooked me up with a psychotherapist/exercise physiologist named Gar who recommended that I spend less time yawning and more time focusing on physical activities that stimulate me, such as baseball. So I went to a Dodgers game, and my back never felt better.

. ♀ 🏆 ♀ .

Be forewarned: I write angry when I'm tired, and I'm writing this at a most ungodly hour when damn near everyone else, save convenience store clerks and speed freaks, is fast asleep under the covers, dreaming about Johnny Depp . . . and yeah, I mean the guys, too! The Depp thing reminds me of something I learned once from a Kentucky woman drinking something called a Sloe Gin Fizz:* there are two final stages to a sexual relationship—the part where you wish/imagine your partner is somebody much better looking and glamorous than she is, and the final-final part where you wish/imagine YOU are somebody much better looking and glamorous than you are.

So I should be asleep, but I'm wide awake, partly because I still put stock in such old-fashioned journalistic principles as meeting deadlines, and partly because I'm still hung up on the whole getting-old thing. But mostly I'm wide awake due to the strident late-night vocal stylings of yet *another* troublesome neighbor, who henceforth will spitefully be referred to as the Screamer, who performs with a percussion accompaniment best described as headboard bongos. Just as I wrote this she hit a note higher than any I've heard since my cousin Dennis had that bicycle-seat incident on Moab's Slickrock Trail. That was followed by a scream that sounded for all the world like the remixed screech of a misadjusted fan belt combined with that sound a dial-up modem makes when it hits connection pay dirt.

The Screamer just moved in recently, and Bottomfeeder saw her first. After he told me she was a serious JAPA ("Jessica Alba–like Piece of Ass"), I spent countless hours patrolling the corridor hoping to bump into her. Yes, ladies, most of us really are that pathetic, and the fine line between "chance encounter" and "stalking" can be no more than

---

* A seductive variation of the just-hit-legal-drinking-age standard calls for a half ounce each of sloe gin (Hiram Walker or Mr. Boston), Southern Comfort, vodka, Galliano, and Frangelico. Shake it all up with roughly five ounces of OJ, and pour over ice in a highball glass.

a question of timing and style. Oh, and in case you're wondering how Sylvia might play into this, for now let's just say she split almost as abruptly as she'd reappeared. I'll offer more on this development later in the book.

So I wound up welcoming the Screamer to the neighborhood and giving her a quick rundown of its amenities—as if occasionally being able to find street parking within five blocks of the building qualifies as an amenity—and I may have made a joke or two about the steep penalty for being late with the rent. . . . Geez, I gotta get some new material.

Truth is, I didn't know what in the world I actually said to the gal when we first met because throughout the entire conversation what I was really listening to was the little voice in my head—the one I call Cyrano de Brainiac, who feeds smooth lines to my subconscious . . . carefully crafted lines that damn near always net me a game of mattress hockey. I think Cyrano had me ask if her necklace was handmade, because it sure looked much like some tribal crafts I'd seen in Bora Bora that time Sting* hosted the mountain-climbing party . . . stuff like that.

But alas, not even Cyrano could put that puck in play. And it had everything to do with what transpired at the End of my conversation with the Screamer, which I remember quite well. It went like this:

---

* When I met Sting at a party at the 2006 Sundance Film Festival, I remarked that he and I were most likely the only two people in the room who'd been at the Police reunion at Giants Stadium during the 1986 Amnesty International tour, to which Sting replied, "That wasn't me, that was my grandfather." Sting is really cool!

Me: "So, maybe after you get settled in and all, I could officially welcome you to the neighborhood by buying you a drink. There's a great little karaoke bar up the street. You can't beat the Anchor Steam* on tap, and I do a pretty mean rendition of 'Satisfaction.'"

Her: "That sounds great. . . ."

⚡ Red Bull-shit ⚡

I'm no fan of mixing Red Bull or any other barely legal stimulant with vodka, because I've found the resulting cocktails not only taste like soiled toilet paper, but may also send misleading signals about my sexuality (technically, I'm what the doctors call "frigid"). In the past, this energy-drink aversion has proved problematic whenever I've been out on the town tippling and in serious need of a quick jolt of energy. And before you even go there, bear in mind that I'm unequivocally opposed to drug use these days, having barely survived five punishing years living in a decadent resort town where certain narcotics are so prevalent it was not uncommon to find some of the seedier local businesses closed for snow days during the most sweltering dog days of summer.

So just imagine how excited I felt to discover p.i.n.k., the world's first 80-proof vodka infused with caffeine and Guarana. Named for the Guarani tribe in Brazil, where the plant that yields it is found in abundance, Guarana is a berry that when consumed affects the body like caffeine laced with speed. Many people believe it cures headaches and induces weight loss, and the Guarani have been using it for centuries to combat bowel disease. Okay, so who's ready for a Cosmo?

A company rep told me that p.i.n.k.'s unusual spelling hints at a secret that has to do with the process of removing the dark color and bitter flavor from the Guarana. Eh, whatever . . . the bottom line is, p.i.n.k. compares favorably with other premium vodkas in taste and price, and it's a godsend for buzz-seekers who can't stomach Red Bull. Plus, if the Guarani are correct, drinking it might forestall that awful day when Depends undergarments become de rigueur.

---

* San Francisco's tastiest and most famous brew has been around since 1896, the year Sting was born.

. . . *She lied.* At least I think she was lying. She had to be, cuz chicks don't drink Anchor Steam; it's too heavy for them. As far as I can tell, women in the twenty-first century have abandoned beer altogether in favor of crap such as vodka mixed with **Red Bull**. Still, I like to throw that out as a test reel—to see if they bite regardless. If they do, I'm "in" like a Madonna record at a gay bar. But you get the point: chick says yes to an Anchor Steam while you butcher a Stones classic, and she's digging you something proper. Unless, of course . . .

Her: "Do you mind if my boyfriend comes along?"

You're Fucking-A right I do! What do I look like, the damn Welcome Wagon?

Me: Boyfriend? No . . . I mean, sure, bring him along . . . but I've gotta get going now . . . something's . . . wrong . . . with . . . the . . . parking. I'll, um, call you about that beer sometime.

With that I retreated back into the apartment, a defeated man. But I got over it. Until that night, that is. That night I discovered that not only was the Screamer's boyfriend inconveniently* still alive, he was apparently packing more beef stick than a Hickory Farms factory worker. Either that, or he was doing things most men hadn't even *considered* yet. It was the only explanation for the sound he made her

---

* at least as far as I was concerned

make when she came—a three-minute refrain that sounded like maybe three hundred cats fighting in a giant sack.

So maybe making a play on the Screamer is worth rethinking, despite her JAPA status. Sure, she sounds like a real hellcat in the sack, but I live next door—a hookup could only lead to big trouble. Instead, I may just hook six or seven digital mikes to my wall, download the sounds of her sexual escapades to my laptop, and lay down a few rap lyrics.

As this chapter is supposed to be about the Ladies, I'm willing to share some very personal information with you regarding my mating philosophy: although I desire women at least as passionately as George Hamilton craves sunshine, and have over the years connected with some breathtakingly stone-cold foxes, my on again–off again girlfriend Sylvia among them, never once have I seriously considered getting **married**. And I doubt I ever will. I don't particularly have anything against the institution, mind you, it's just that I don't believe I've yet squeezed all the enjoyment out of the Bachelor Life and that continuing to do so may turn out to be a lifelong endeavor. Being a raffish single dude is a real gas, and I plan on riding it out until the thrill is gone . . . if indeed that day ever comes. Granted, there was a time when I began to grow weary of the redundancy of the pickup process. Pretending to enjoy Oprah *and* Ellen just so women might deem me sensitive had gotten old. Embellishing my career and lying about my income turned a bore.

Ditto on recycling tarradiddles about the places I'd been and the famous people I knew. As for feigning interest in their lives, well, that became unbearably dull. Things got so bad that most nights I could barely muster the energy to get off the barstool and comb the environs for the easiest drunk gal in the place. Desperate for a

---

🍻 Married Guy's Day Out 🍻

No matter how "happily married" a guy purports to be, my research has shown that there are times when it is impossible for even the most uxorious hubby to escape his inner frat boy. When that happens, at best the Married Guy (MG) escapes with a nasty hangover and the nagging suspicion that his wife thinks he's a buffoon. At worst, those moments prove a prelude to divorce. Here's how the typical "Married Guy's day out" scenario might play:

10:15 AM—MG kisses his wife lovingly as she heads off to yoga class. He promises he won't drink too many beers this time and that he'll be home right after the big game.

10:16 AM—While passing a mirror, MG notices that his nose has grown eight inches.

10:37 AM—MG's buddy Turbo calls to remind him not to forget to bring the blow-up doll to the tailgate party.

10:48 AM—Having secured shoulder pads, football jersey, and helmet onto said doll, inspiration strikes and MG adds those little black stripes beneath his eyes using his wife's Chanel eyeliner.

10:52 AM—Begins loading cooler with beer.

10:54 AM—Takes a break from loading cooler to crack open the first of what will be an unthinkable number of cold boys.

11:17 AM—While driving to Turbo's place, MG realizes he's forgotten something very important: namely, that driving drunk is a crime.* He puts down his beer, pulls over, starts hitchhiking.

continued on next page >>

* The offense carries many names and acronyms, depending upon the jurisdiction. The most common is Driving Under the Influence (DUI), followed in no particular order by Driving While Impaired (DWI), Driving While Intoxicated (DWI), Operating a Motor Vehicle While Intoxicated (OMVI), and Driving While Passed Out Drunk Behind the Wheel (RIP).

12:22 PM—MG finally catches a ride with a toothless trucker named Cougar who has room for the cooler and the blow-up doll.

12:46 PM—The two of them stop off at a strip club, sneak in beers.

2:33 PM—MG asks a dancer named Brandee to marry him. Tries to explain away presence of wedding ring. Slips her a hundo with his home number scrawled on it. Orders more beer.

3:07 PM—While passing a mirror, MG notices that his nose is redder than Khrushchev-era Communism.

5:36 PM—Flat broke, MG gets tossed from the strip club for trying to steal tips from G-strings.

5:40 PM—MG discovers Cougar in the truck's cab, making it with the blow-up doll. He vomits.

5:43 PM—In a moment of devastating clarity, MG realizes he's missed the game, blown his mortgage payment on lap dances, lost his cell phone, car, blow-up doll, and cooler, and is stranded twenty miles from a home he's probably going to lose in the divorce settlement.

6:00 PM—Despondent, MG is about to purposely step into oncoming traffic when he feels something in his jacket pocket. It's an unopened beer! All is right in the universe . . . until tomorrow morning.

change of pace, I experimented with a variety of novel ways to score dates. First I gave honesty a try, which as you can no doubt imagine yielded disastrous results. The Real Me just isn't all that desirable, no matter how much alcohol is involved. Playing hard to get didn't pan out, either, because that strategy calls for a woman with a desire to get me in the first place. I came up empty with Internet dating as well, mostly because the "F" key on my laptop has a tendency to stick.

Then one night on the dance floor at a trendy L.A. nightclub, as I was about to reach into my Bag of Bullshit and pull out a timeworn yet trusty old nugget—I believe it was, "Is there an airport nearby or is that just my heart taking off?"—inspiration struck. "Shake it, sugar," I cooed to an attractive redhead in a devilish blue dress. "Shake it like a Polaroid picture. . . . Heeeeeeey yaaaa! Heeey ya!!!" And shake it she did, just like the fella from OutKast knew she would when he penned that line, and the Song Lyric Inducement Method (SLIME) was born. Although I didn't get lucky every time out, there's no doubt SLIME breathed new life into the womanizing ways of this Playa Pimp. From the beginning, I've been well served by, "Don't be so quick to walk away, dance with me, I wanna rock your body," because—let's face it—young women drink up that Justin Timberlake nonsense like appletinis. *Why* they dig the effeminate ex-N'Syncer so much, well, I don't get it. But when it comes to cribbing his lyrics to woo women, oh, boy, do I ever get it. Over and over again. Haven't been so lucky going old school. Used the chorus from "Take My Breath Away" on a gal at the gym and it was a total embarrassment. Trust me, it's probably best to refrain from using songs by Berlin or anything at all off the *Top Gun* soundtrack, for that matter. I know a guy who said he met his future wife after belting out Kenny Loggins's "Danger Zone" at a karaoke bar in Cleveland. They divorced after six weeks. Heavy stuff such as Marilyn Manson and Korn are also off-limits, but you can get away with Nine Inch Nails if the hit-upon has serious self-esteem issues, and even then only if it's something off *The Downward Spiral.*

Frankly, the most effective way to SLIME a potential paramour is to borrow from a master hip-hop crooner like Usher or Prince. One time I walked up on a fine-looking hottie in a coffee shop and whispered, "You make me wanna leave the one I'm with to start a new relationship with you." Took her back to my place later that night, and before I could say, "I would die 4 U," we were buck nekked on my water bed fffffffffffffffffffffff . . . damn! There goes that sticky key again.

While scoping the singles scene in bars, I regularly indulge my mischievous inner child by ordering cocktails with such provocative names as Sex on the Beach (a Madras, with peach schnapps) and Slippery Nipple (Baileys, Kahlúa, and butterscotch schnapps). Some of the most superbly sublime moments in my illustrious nightlife career have involved tomfoolery along the lines of roguishly asking attractive barmistresses for a Long Kiss Goodnight (vanilla vodka and crème de cacao) or Their Phone Number (a scowl and a double-shot of cold rejection served straight up). And silly sexual innuendo isn't the only fun to be had when ordering drinks when you're at the bar picking up women instead of, say, at home being married. In fact, there's a vodka from Holland that could be the greatest thing to happen to smartasses since the invention of plastic dog shit and whoopee cushions. It's called Effen, and it is pronounced precisely as it's spelled. As in, "Hey, bartender, can I get some Effen vodka in this drink?" or, "This is the best Effen vodka I've ever tasted," or, "Man, what in the Effen hell was I thinking when I signed on to write a sixty-thousand-word book?"* See how much fun can be had?

Of course, the fun is often followed by a wicked hangover the next morning. . . . But fret not, kids, cuz I got you covered BIG TIME! A few years back I discovered First Call, whose manufacturer bills it as "the only all-natural food product currently on the market for

* For those of you keeping score at home, the word count to this point is **43,017**.

hangover prevention." The only one, huh? I remember thinking to myself, *Guess the folks over at First Call haven't heard of a little all-natural food product called the Bloody Mary.* Still, with a long European "booze junket" in the offing, I decided to give First Call a shot. The capsules are made entirely from the edible part of the hybrid artichoke and sarsaparilla root, and aid in the elimination of toxins in the liver. The regimen is simple: take three capsules prior to drinking, and three more just before you pass out on the hotel room floor (or wherever you wind up after a night on the town). I popped the pills, shared several bottles of Veuve Clicquot with a Hungarian supermodel, and woke up in the Presidential Suite of a tony boutique hotel. And I gotta tell ya, friends, I felt sprightlier than a puppy . . . without all the drool. Just to be sure it wasn't a fluke, I repeated the process the following evening—this time with some highly potent single-malt Scotch and a rather unstable exotic dancer named Siobhan. Next day, I woke up and ran three miles! *

This is probably a good time to point out that drinking and womanizing don't always go hand in shaky hand. One incident in particular comes to mind: I was several hours into what was shaping up to be a splendid evening down at a local watering hole, JP's Bar & Grill. A scrumptious little number named Betty was eating up my tall tales of adventure on the high seas—I'd recently seen *The Pirates of the Caribbean* movie—and Kelly the bartender had completely forgotten about a rather large outstanding bar tab. Plus, Bottomfeeder was

---

* Turns out, that stripper was really crazy . . . and fast.

nowhere in sight, and the Misfits were playing on the jukebox. It was a good night, to be sure. Intent on polishing off what had to be my sixth or seventh Knob Creek and ginger ale, I carelessly raised the highball glass to my lips . . . and that's when I made a painful discovery about the incredible amount of damage a stiff drinking straw can inflict upon the fragile human eye.

Lying on a gurney in the emergency room at the hospital, it dawned on me just how precarious a devotion to nightlife can be. Bars generally tend to be filled with drunk people who smoke, handle glassware, and, most alarmingly, open their mouths to speak—often to complete strangers whom they are trying to convince to come home with them. Yes, the average drinking establishment is a veritable breeding ground for mishaps. If you think about it, bar accidents occur all the time, from the relatively harmless chipped tooth caused by overenthusiastically sucking on a beer bottle to the downright dangerous "elbow slip," which has led many an over-lubricated taverngoer to face-plant onto the bar and/or floor. It's a wonder more of us aren't incapacitated.

Men who don't wear underwear or button-fly jeans are likely all too familiar with the agony associated with a "careless zip-up" in the john. Then there are those embarrassing "piss stains" due to insufficient shaking.* And how many of us have forgotten to wash our hands after grabbing hold of a grubby toilet handle, only to come

---

* Nightlife Tip #224: Although no longer considered stylish by fashionistas, acid-washed jeans quite effectively camouflage pee-pee marks.

down later with a wicked case of hepatitis? Whew, I know I've been *there* before.

The "drunk drop" is a common mishap that occurs when a person's grip is weakened by the presence of excessive amounts of booze. Usually the dropper doesn't even realize that he/she is no longer holding a drink until the next attempted sip, compounding the embarrassment and/or risk of injury. Toes and feet, incidentally, are most at risk in a "drunk dropping" incident. Not very hazardous if it involves a twelve-ounce Miller Lite, but anything heavier, like, say, a Foster's oil can or a pint of Smithwick's, and the victim could spend weeks hobbling around like a retired NFL lineman.

"Misstepping" is another common bar-related calamity. Liberal doses of substances such as tequila and gin often have a blurring effect on a person's field of vision, and can actually cause the limbs to behave erratically. That's when two steps begin to look like three steps, and climbing five steps feels like seven steps. Of course, if you find yourself "misstepping" with any regularity, it may be time to consider entering a program involving twelve steps. "Drunken singing" is a disaster that happens all too frequently in bars, especially those that feature Neil Diamond and Abba on the jukebox. Invariably, fights break out, ears are permanently damaged, and some lout mangles the words to "Pour Some Sugar on Me."

And finally, the "inappropriate remark" loudly blurted at the exact moment that everyone else in the bar suddenly goes silent can have some serious repercussions. Lord knows that in the wake of a serious beating incurred a few years ago at a biker bar in Phoenix, I'll think twice before uttering the words "I'd like to bang the bouncer's wife" ever again.

In addition to hangovers, damaged retinas, broken toes, shattered egos, nicked willies, and tools hitting on you with cheesy song
lyrics, one of the biggest nuisances associated with the Drinking Life
is that sometimes an uncontrollable urge for a good buzz comes on
at a most inopportune time . . . such as on the day before payday,
when most boozers are flat-ass broke. That's when the hard-core
types usually turn to cost-efficient concoctions that really have no
business being put into the human body. Once, when my wallet was
especially weightless, I tried something called a "White-Trash
Russian," a dreadful combination of Bowman's Virginia vodka and
Yoo-hoo. I'm almost certain it did some irreparable damage to my
stomach lining and, quite possibly, my central nervous system. I had
to drink seltzer and pop Tums for several weeks afterwards just to
get right again. The experience did get me to thinking, though. What
are the best poor-man's cocktails? Surely, not every cheap drink out
there tastes like Sterno. I see guys in tank tops drinking out of Sty-
rofoam cups while munching on pigs in a blanket and cheese puffs at
the local municipal park on Saturday afternoons . . . and they look so
goddamn happy. What's in those cups?

"The 'Poor Man's Margarita'—tequila and Squirt—is a popular
one out West," says my pal Terry Sullivan. "And in some eastern cities,
large parties used to get by on 'Purple Passions'—Welch's grape juice
and grain alcohol. But I hear that 'Blue Lagoons'—whatever that blue
sports drink crap is, plus grain alcohol—have recently supplanted
them in some circles." Cash-strapped drunks in Chicago swear by
"Muddy Bottoms," a potent combination of Green River "gourmet"
soda and cheap bourbon. And I've heard that during the great urine-test

scare a few years back, some less-than-tasteful folks in Denver used to serve a lovely thing called "Pee in the Bottle"—Mountain Dew and vodka or Everclear in plastic specimen cups. Served *warm*—for verisimilitude. Some of the curb-sitters in my old neighborhood in Philadelphia used to specialize in what was known as the "Colt Python" (from the handgun of the same name) by adding a couple of shots of whatever cheap blended whiskey was on sale at the state store to a half quart of Colt 45 malt liquor. So now you *really* know what they mean by the old phrase "pick your poison."

<u>Step 9</u>

Brushes with Celebrities, Comb-Overs with Nobodies

"So," asked the pretty gal on the other side of the desk, "are you really the Imbiber?"

"Uh, maybe...yeah," I mumbled. Over the years I'd come to adopt a fair measure of wariness toward that question, but then again my photos were easily accessible in the newspaper as well as on my Web site,* not to mention that I was wearing a "Read *The Imbiber* and Nobody Gets Hurt" T-shirt.† Plausible deniability à la FDR and Nixon was pretty much out of the question. "Wow! I read your column every week in *Metro*. I can't believe you're really THE IMBIBER!" she more or less gushed.

I was trying to get in to see David Steinberger, President and CEO of Perseus Books. I wanted to discuss his company's recent acquisition of Avalon Publishing Group and any possible ramifications the merger might have on the publication, promotion, and sales strategy of my book.

---

* www.theimbiber.net

† Available in all sizes at www.theimbiber.net.

I was also hoping to score a comp copy of Michael Eric Dyson's latest best seller about the black experience in America.* I'd gotten as far as Steinberger's executive assistant's summer intern's temp, the young lady who turned out to be such an unabashed fan of my weekly spirits screed. Her excitement was understandable. After all, she thought she was speaking with the Imbiber. I didn't have the heart to tell her that it was just me, Danny Dunn, the mere channel for my larger-than-life alter ego.

In truth, it often seems that the Imbiber is some sort of otherworldly being who intermittently takes over my body, exerting absolute control over it to sate his own voracious appetite for pleasure. Nocturnal in the way that other people are Freewill Baptists, the Imbiber usually shows up hell-bent on wreaking havoc at night, after Danny Dunn's consciousness has been weakened by some combination of alcohol, sleep deprivation, and chronically low self-esteem. The differences between the two of us can be striking.

Whenever the opportunity presents itself—and in the glamorous world of professional spirits reportage, it does so regularly—the Imbiber sets up shop on a barstool at some trendy haunt where he knocks back snifter after snifter of wildly expensive hootch the caliber of Martell Creation Grand Extra cognac† while bragging about all the exotic places he's visited to gaggles of female admirers susceptible to the lure of a good yarn and some potent liquor. Danny Dunn wakes

---

* I was still reeling from the Blake Shipley debacle.

† An exquisite blend from the oldest of the major cognac houses, made up of the finest eaux-de-vie aged in Troncais barrels instead of the Limousin oak variety favored by the majority of other producers: three hundred dollars a bottle.

up the next morning in bed with a total stranger, a wicked hangover, and the faint recollection of yet another appalling bar tab.

The Imbiber hitches rides on private jets for weekend getaways to Anguilla, where he hobnobs with folks whose last names appear on one's kitchen appliances. Welcome by name at the most exclusive clubs on the international jet-set circuit, he's always in the company of some powerful group or individual who welcomes his casual wisdom on matters of the highest import. Danny Dunn, however, struggles with the ethical implications of shoplifting bean burritos from the 7-11 at 4:00 AM.

"So, Mr. Imbiber," the cutie jolted me out of my rumination, "you should write something about what it's like to work in an office at a big place like Perseus. . . . That'd be interesting, huh?"

"SURE, OR MAYBE I'LL TAKE IT ONE STEP FURTHER AND POSTULATE ON WHAT IT'D BE LIKE TO COUNT MY FINGERS AND TOES FOR A LIVING!" Clearly, and without warning, the Imbiber had taken over.*

"Excuse me?" she said.

"LOOK, BABE, IF YOU WANT AN ARTICLE ABOUT BEING A SLAB RAT FOR A FACELESS CONGLOMERATE, WHY DON'T *YOU* WRITE IT?!" he jeered. "I'M SURE THE BIG MAGAZINES WOULD PAY BEAUCOUP BUCKS FOR A FRESH IDEA LIKE THAT!!!"

"Sheesh, I'm sorry I said anything," she grumbled, sliding a clipboard in front of the boor. "Sign in and have a seat over there."

---

* He's what's known as an ALL CAPS personality.

"NO, WAIT, I'M SORRY I WAS RUDE," he whispered softly, leaning ever so slightly into her personal space. "I'VE BEEN UNDER SUCH STRESS SINCE MY KITTEN, SNOOKUMS, WAS DIAGNOSED WITH RICKETS."

"Oh, the poor kitty," she said gently, placing a consoling hand atop his own.

"I KNOW, I KNOW . . . IT'S BEEN VERY, VERY HARD. EVER SINCE I FOUND HER ABANDONED IN A DUMPSTER AND NURSED HER BACK TO HEALTH, SNOOKUMS HAS BEEN LIKE FAMILY," he said, choking up for effect. "AND THEN THERE'S THE PRESSURE OF DELIVERING THE BOOK ON TIME, AND KEEPING UP WITH ALL MY VOLUNTEER WORK, AND . . . AND . . . SAY, WHY DON'T WE MEET LATER FOR A DRINK SO WE CAN FLESH OUT YOUR OFFICE STORY IDEA?"

She lit up. "Really? You'd do that for me?"

"ABSOLUTELY . . . OH, WAIT . . . DARN, I'M AFRAID I CAN'T. I'M A LITTLE SHORT ON CASH THIS WEEK, WHAT WITH SNOOKUMS'S VET BILL AND MY CHARI-TABLE DONATIONS AND ALL," he said, patting his empty wallet for emphasis.

Of course, the executive assistant's secretary's intern or whatever she was agreed to meet for a drink *and* foot the bill. She was a stunner, and the Imbiber decided that the most effective means of wooing her would be to continue to pour on the "sensitive guy" routine. From somewhere in the surreal netherworld where I'm exiled whenever HE takes over, I could swear I heard him coo, "PLEASE BE GENTLE; I'VE BEEN HURT BEFORE."

⋅ 𝚈 𝐘 𝚈 ⋅

There are a number of people like the secretary at Perseus who know my name and have at least a passing familiarity with my work in the newspaper. By no means am I famous, but I do meet lots of celebrities, and have developed a knack for glomming onto them in order to revel in the trappings of fame by association. For the past several years now, I've kept the network intact by hosting a holiday shindig for my "**Hollywood friends**," almost all of whom have unusual names. I came up with the idea while perched on a barstool at O'Brien's, arguing with Bottomfeeder over the artistic merits of our mutual acquaintance Chaka Khan. It turns out that my insufferable roomie was a roadie on Chaka's 1992 *The Woman I Am* tour. I knew her through a deejay friend of mine named Mixmaster Nose Ring, who'd done an infectious remix of "Ain't Nobody" that was a bona fide smash on the gay club circuit back in the early Clinton years.

One thing led to another, and on an unusually chilly L.A. evening in December of 2003, I wound up having Chaka, Nose Ring, his good friend actor-comedian Cheech Marin, and Charo over for pomegranate martinis* and cocktail wieners. And boy, was it ever a hoot— particularly the discordant discourse between a liquored-up Chaka, Cheech, and Charo. Great stuff. Really. And the thing just kinda grew from there.

---

* The recipe I normally use comes courtesy of 44, the chic lobby lounge at the Royalton Hotel in midtown Manhattan. Made with Patrón Silver tequila, Cointreau, fresh lime and pomegranate juice, this refreshing concoction is like sweet mariachi music for the mouth, if you can imagine what that might taste like. Substituting mango puree for the pomegranate juice yields a version with a little more tang to it. Tang, by the way, is my third-favorite word in the English language.

⚡ Farewell to a Fife ⚡

Regrettably, the legendary actor Don Knotts never attended one of my holiday parties. Knotts, best known for his role as Deputy Barney Fife on *The Andy Griffith Show*, passed away in February 2006, and while the rest of the so-called Hollywood media mourned or slept or chased Brad Pitt and Angelina Jolie and their adopted kids around impoverished Third World countries, *Entertainment Tonight* was on the case in search of what they dubbed "the lost Don Knotts tapes." That's right—the lost Don Knotts tapes! Knotts died on Friday, February 24, and at the top of the syndicated show the following Monday a bleary-eyed Mary Hart—who'd clearly been turning over stones all weekend long—revealed that the lost Don Knotts tapes had, in fact, been recovered and that *ET* had the exclusive.

As anyone with even a passing knowledge of showbiz lore knows, the whereabouts of these tapes—which contain footage of Don Knotts shaking his *Three's Company* co-star Joyce DeWitt's hand at a backstage birthday bash—had long been one of Hollywood's greatest mysteries, alongside other monumental head-scratchers such as the source of George Hamilton's fame and the decision to make Grace Jones a Bond Girl. Indeed, not since Clara Peller begged the profound question, "Where's the beef?" had inquiring minds been so flummoxed.

In tribute to Don Knotts and the investigative reporting prowess of *ET*, I would like to propose a toast—in shot form, because Don would have wanted it that way—that the folks in Mayberry, and maybe even down at the Regal Beagle, would've surely enjoyed. It's called a Barney on Acid, and while I can't say for sure that it's named for Knotts's beloved bungling lawman, I do know this—had Barney Fife ever actually *done* acid, it would have made for the funniest *Andy Griffith Show* ever. Who knows, maybe the lost "Barney is tripping" episode is out there waiting to be found. Somebody get Mary Hart on the line!

Barney on Acid
0.5 oz. blue curacao
0.5 oz. Jägermeister
splash of cranberry juice

Shake with ice and strain into a shot glass.

Last year's event was the biggest yet, with a guest list that included Chaka, Cheech, Charo, and Cher, along with U2 guitarist The Edge,

The Rock, Chris Rock, Kid Rock, and former adult superstar Rock Steadie. Chastity Bono, Bono, Bon Jovi, and the guy who played Boner on Growing Pains showed up, as did all four Zappa kids—Moon Unit, Ahmet Rodan, Diva, and Dweezil—along with the surviving members of the acting Phoenix clan: Joaquin, Summer, Rain, and Liberty. Slash, Screech, Sade, Seal, and Sisqo found themselves hobnobbing with Prince, Queen Latifah, and the King Ad Rock. Tiger, Tyra, Tyrese, and Treach stopped by, but none of them stayed long because they had tickets to see Carrot Top. Moby, Iggy Pop, and Marilyn Manson were no-shows, but that's okay because Fat Boy Slim brought along his turntable, much to the delight of Keanu, Kiefer, Kutcher, Kieran, and Macaulay Culkin ... music lovers all. Too bad Sir Mix-a-Lot was a no-show, because "Baby Got Back" is a rad party tune.*

As you can imagine, there were plenty of fascinating conversations and spirited debates. For instance, Moon Unit, Summer, Slash, the Edge, and I argued for nearly half an hour over who was the most unusually named Stooge. We finally settled on Shemp (with the Edge dissenting; he's a big Curly Joe fan). And Dweezil Zappa—always the joker—amused himself and others by periodically shouting, "Hey, Rock!" across the room, then watching Chris, Kid, King Ad, and The all turn around.

Things got a little crazy around midnight when Bottomfeeder, who'd gone out for more beer and some bug spray (Flea was getting

---

* I cannot be dishonest about my affinity for big butts, and I love watching a crowd of well-lubricated revelers go ass-out crazy the moment they hear, "Oh my God, Becky, look at her butt. It's so big."

out of hand), burst in shouting, "Zsa Zsa struck the concierge in the lobby!"

"Wait a minute," I shot back. "We don't have a lobby or a concierge . . . and what the hell is Zsa Zsa doing here?!"

"I invited her because Sisqo wanted to meet her," he said. "But that's not important. The point is, she smacked somebody on the way up here, and now the police are out front with their weapons drawn!"

I went downstairs and cleared things up with the cops. Turns out Zsa Zsa lost her notorious temper when a neighbor of mine, the actor Jake Gyllenhaal, had the audacity to try to share an elevator with her and her toy poodle. Took off her glove and whipped it across his face— normally a pretty harmless way to assault someone, but in this case, Zsa Zsa was wearing diamond-encrusted leather gloves and one of the big rocks caught Jake in the eye and detached his retina. Word on the street is he may be permanently impaired. Of course, the whole incident got me down. After all, what sort of unusual-name-party-planner am I if I leave a guy with a name like Gyllenhaal off the invite list? Oh well, there's always next year.

And that reminds me—I need to get Coolio's phone number.

* ⚱ 🏆 ⚱ *

Although we've never been introduced, I did happen to be in close quarters once with Larry King at an advance screening of *The Passion of the Christ* on the Sony lot in Culver City, California. Larry was sitting next to a hot youngish blonde whom I assumed to be his latest wife. Larry didn't look good, either. Not sick or anything, just not good. He's an unattractive man with a disproportionately large head topped by hair the consistency of hay. There was a gay dude with Larry and the blonde, and as we waited for the film to begin, he made repeated attempts to steer the conversation toward same-sex marriage. Larry was having none of that, however, and instead loudly and randomly remarked that God made marijuana. Since we were about to see *The Passion of the Christ*, almost everyone in the screening room seemed to feel the need to discuss God, but Larry King was the only one talking about His role in the creation of loco weed. I was thinking Larry was the absolute bomb at that point, but I was in the minority. People shot him angry looks. Many were clearly put off by the suggestion that God created pot—true as that certainly is—but no one actually said anything to Larry King because, well, he's Larry-fucking-King. The gay dude remarked that the mayor of San Francisco is a hero, but Larry cut him off to tell the blonde she was a bad driver.

"Well, then you drive next time, Larry," she snapped. "Hah!" he cackled loudly. Then, if my booze-soaked memory is correct,* Larry suddenly lost consciousness and slumped forward, his giant head flattening a tub of popcorn. But then just like that, he popped up again and cackled some more.

Seated beside me was a movie critic from *LA Weekly* who informed me that one of Mel Gibson's earliest decisions as director of *The Passion of the Christ* was to have the Jesus of his film speak Aramaic, the same language that the historical Jesus spoke two thousand

---

* It isn't.

years ago. At this, I mentioned that I was taking a beginners' Spanish class at my local community college.

"Oh, you'll love learning Spanish," the critic gushed. "It's a beautiful language."

I told him I was already fluent in Spanish, and that I had enrolled merely in order to feed my appetite for superiority. No one could deny that I was the best student in the class.

"Do you think Larry King is stoned right now?" I asked, eyeing the blonde lasciviously. I was pretty sure I loved her. The *LA Weekly* critic got up and moved to another seat. Then I was really bored, so I pulled out my cell phone, flipped it open, held it high, and pointed it toward the blank screen. A burly security guard rushed over and demanded to see the phone, so I gave it to him.

"It's turned off," he said, studying it intently.

"That's correct," I replied.

"Well, then why were you holding it up?"

"I was admiring the craftsmanship. The Japanese really make quality electronic devices, doncha think?"

This threw him off balance. He carried himself like a marine, this guy, and I'd swear I heard him whistling a Toby Keith tune out in the lobby. It had to just tear him apart to be cashing paychecks from Sony.

"You can't hold the phone up like that," he barked with finality.

"Sure you can. I just did, and nobody's any worse off because of it, right?" Then I moved in close and whispered, "Look, man, you might want to keep an eye on that guy up there with the big head."

"Larry King?"

"Yes, Larry King!" I said, my voice rising ever so slightly. "He's twisted!"

"Twisted?"

"Without a doubt," I hissed. "On pot or something worse! He's been haranguing that young woman next to him since he arrived!"

"Are you sure?" the guard asked, his anxiety bubbling to the surface. "I mean, he looks pretty calm and he is . . . uh . . . he is *Larry King*."

I grabbed the guard forcefully by the lapels and pulled him in tight. He was rattled now; his expression betrayed anger and fear. "He's not calm, he's in a drug-induced trance! And yeah, he's Larry King all right, but this movie is about God our almighty savior! It's goddamn sacrilege what that bowling-ball-headed talking head is doing up there, man!"

"You're right," he said. "I've got to throw him out of here."

"He's really left you with no other choice," I replied, rising from my seat. "But you better let me go with you—to comfort that poor blonde."

"His wife?"

"Well, maybe not for long," I said, digging through my pockets for a breath mint. Then I handed the guard my business card. "By the way, I may split early and get her to a hotel so we, er, she can lie down and recover. . . . Do me a favor—give me a jingle and let me know how the movie ends."

· ♈ 🍸 ♈ ·

On many occasions your liquor-nipping correspondent has partied like a champ, but until I met Sugar Ray Leonard I'd never actually partied *with* one. Ah, but anything's possible in the effulgent desert-dry den of iniquity that is Las Vegas, especially in the wee hours of the morning in the Shadow Bar at Caesar's Palace, which is where I found myself in the winter of 2006 hunkered down in a private booth next to the legendary boxer. The Hall of Fame pugilist hadn't fought professionally in quite some time, his last win coming back in 1989 against Roberto Duran. But the guy appeared to be in tip-top shape, and I suspected that if push ever came to punch he'd mop the floor with every one of the young boxers who'd appeared on the Leonard-hosted TV show *The Contender* or, without a doubt, a mouthy out-of-shape booze writer. So it was with a fair amount of trepidation (and beer muscles) that I called the champ out on what I observed to be some surprisingly lightweight drinking habits.

"*No mas!*" I shouted, harking back to Ray's most memorable encounter with Duran, although I was referring to the Cape Codders* he was ordering.

"What's wrong with Cape Codders? I really enjoy them," the champ replied, instantly topping my list of Top 10 Things I Never Thought I'd Hear a Guy Who Kicked Marvin Hagler's Ass Say.†

"You're one of the toughest fighters of all time, man. You should

---

* Vodka, cranberry juice, and a lime wedge . . . duh!

† Okay, so maybe it wasn't a complete ass-whupping. In their one and only meeting inside the ring, an April 1987 contest known simply as "The Fight," Leonard beat the heavily favored Hagler in a controversial split decision.

be drinking something harder than Cape Codders! Can I interest you in a Rusty Nail, perhaps?"*

"Well," Sugar Ray said thoughtfully, "I like chardonnay a lot, too."† It dawned on me that it was only a matter of time before the words "Shirley Temple" came out of the mouth of the guy who once TKO'd Tommy "The Hitman" Hearns,° and I didn't want to see Ray go out like that. Word was spreading that Justin Timberlake was in the bar, and I'd be damned if I was going to sit idly by while Sugar Ray Leonard professed a love of boy bands.

I headed back to L.A. posthaste, but didn't fare much better chatting with J. D. Fortune at Hollywood's House of Blues a few hours after he'd been chosen in front of a national TV audience to be the lead singer of INXS. "If there are words to describe this feeling, I can't find them right now," offered Fortune, who grew up in Canada idolizing the multiplatinum band that was once fronted by the late Michael Hutchence. I hadn't asked J. D. to size up his emotional state, but if he needed to put that out there, well, who was I to quibble? To be honest, I was merely hoping to have a few drinks on the band's tab

---

* Scotch, Drambuie, and a lemon peel in an ice-filled old-fashioned glass

† Try Newton Unfiltered Chardonnay 2003 ($50): it's pricey, but worth every penny. The Newton is an impeccable expression of the very best chardonnays Northern California has to offer. Tasting reveals layer upon layer of flavors ranging from butterscotch to citrus to roasted almonds. I can't recommend it highly enough.

° That 1981 bout at Caesar's Palace was dubbed "The Showdown," and Leonard—well behind on all the judges' scorecards—made a miraculous comeback to stop Hearns in the fourteenth round.

and maybe score some leftover babes. What a life, eh? From here on
out, J. D. Fortune gets to party like a rock star FOR A LIVING! Talk
about your killer benefits packages.

"I'm really into infused vodkas and stuff like that," J. D. told me
before he left to go make time with some models. Bah! I thought . . .
I'd had enough with the vodka. Premium, super-premium, ultrapremium, single-batch, mega-distilled, prime-select Grade A
chilly-most . . . who could keep up? For weeks I'd been on a super-
premium light rum kick. Since there was only one on the market at
that time, the choice was simple: **10 Cane**, which is produced on
the windswept isle of Trinidad, and oh, how sweet it is. I got
acquainted with this special spirit at a luncheon held at the posh
Hotel Bel Air. Between mouthfuls of Cuban pressed sandwiches
and chipotle-rubbed tenderloin of beef, I enjoyed the tastiest
mojito I'd had this side of Little Havana. And the 10 Cane daiquiris
were to die for, though I don't recommend it (dying, that is).

10 Cane Daiquiri

2 oz. 10 Cane rum
1 oz. fresh-squeezed lime juice
1 oz. simple syrup
lime wheel for garnish

Shake ingredients with ice. Strain into a chilled cocktail glass and garnish.

Daiquiri in hand, I made my way over to INXS guitarist Tim
Farriss and asked him if he could recall some of the wild times he'd
had as part of one of the world's more famous bands. He told me that
the best nights were usually the ones he couldn't remember. "But there

was this one time in Paris . . ." he said, and I'll leave out the rest as there's still a chance we'll market this as a children's book.

Eventually I'd discover firsthand what it's like to carouse with Farriss. After a party at the home of celebrated TV producer Mark Burnett, Tim and I made our way to a popular beachside hotel in Santa Monica called the Viceroy. We drank **Martin Miller's London Dry Gin**, slurped oysters from the half shell, and handed out Cosmic Kisses* to all the pretty girls. I'm not sure who footed the bill for the extravagance, but it sure as shit wasn't Farriss or me. I'd lost my wallet hours earlier, and famous musicians—by rule—never pay for anything. "Let's have a shot, Danny boy!" I recall Tim shouting. "Another round for everyone!"

〽 Martin Miller Is the Man 〽

Martin Miller's London Dry Gin is the eponymous creation of an English antiques expert who, having grown frustrated over a perceived dearth of quality gins, decided to whip up an ultrapremium of his own. After much trial and error, Miller concocted an 80-proof wonder that has the potential to revolutionize and repopularize gin in much the same way the likes of Grey Goose and Ketel One did for vodka.

Miller seeks out the best botanicals—juniper along with other stuff like cassia bark and Florentine Iris—and distills them in a hundred-year-old copper still dubbed "Grandma." Once the heart of the single batch distillation is extracted, it gets shipped from the UK to Iceland, where it's married with lava-filtered glacial water and bottled. I'm telling you, people, ol' Marty should have called the stuff Baby's Ass instead, cuz it's *that* smooth (and drinking enough of it will get you pretty, uh, crappy). Is it the water? The still? Magic? I dunno, but I can tell you that Miller's gin is so good it was awarded double gold at the 2006 San Francisco World Spirits Competition.

---

* A combination of peach nectar and Moët Nectar Impérial served in a champagne flute.

There are bad ideas, really bad ideas, and then there are the words—almost always uttered with gross intemperance—"Another round of shots." And by shots I'm talking about a straight ounce and a half of a single, robust spirit. Concoctions with names like Attitude Adjustment, Gorilla Fart, or Mind Eraser are not shots, my friends. They're telltale signs that you frequently wet the bed as a child. At the Viceroy we drank Jägermeister or, as I like to call it, the Devil's Bile. Hell, we were downing the stuff like it was 1987 all over again.*

From the Viceroy, with several groupies in tow—Tim's, not mine—we wound up back at my crib, where Tim proceeded to spill an entire bottle of '98 Penfold's Grange† all over my white living room sofa and one of the groupies, who also happened to be quite white. I didn't get nearly as upset as she did, though. On the contrary, I was moved by the spirit of drunken rock star debauchery and summarily tossed an antique electric guitar into the bathtub and lit it on fire, à la Jimi Hendrix at the Monterey Pop Festival.° I believe that's right

---

* 1987 was the high-water mark for sales of both Jägermeister and INXS albums.

† Nightlife Tip #365: When hanging with rich Aussies, drink expensive Aussie wine.

° No fewer than three tracks from Hendrix's incredible 1967 debut album, *Are You Experienced?* were intoxicating enough to have drinks named after them—the most popular being a **Purple Haze**, which is usually prepared one of two ways: either with vodka, blackberry schnapps, and orange juice, or vodka, raspberry liqueur, and 7-Up. A **Foxey Lady** is Amaretto, crème de cacao, and light cream shaken with ice and strained into a cocktail glass. Those with sweet teeth might want to try a **Red House** (Black Haus blackberry schnapps, sloe gin, and cranberry juice). Jimi often made magic playing other artists' music, and one of his most rousing covers was of the Trogg's only hit, "**Wild Thing,**" which appears on several of his live recordings. The drink that bears that name sounds pretty rockin' as well: Tequila, club soda, cranberry juice, and lime juice on the rocks.

about when everyone left. I have a vague recollection of the cops showing up sometime later on. Or maybe it was the fire department. Or both. The lesson here, of course, is never serve red wine on a white sofa, as it can only lead to big trouble.

There's a point, of course, to all this party talk and name-dropping, and that point is that I am having a much better time than most of you. . . . Wait, that's not it—the point is a shot recipe with a name that could make even Tim Farriss turn red:

Fucked by a Rockstar
1 oz. vodka
0.5 oz. Triple Sec
0.5 oz. Rockstar energy drink

Pour the ingredients into a two-ounce shot glass and slam it.

· ♈ ♉ ♈ ·

She may very well be the most overexposed individual on the planet in this young century, and while I certainly wouldn't want to further magnify the spectacle that is Paris Hilton, I'd be remiss if I didn't offer at least a glancing mention of our special evening together in France. I was in the Côte d'Azur covering the 2006 Cannes Film Festival for my employer, Metro International Newspapers, and my editor had made arrangements for me to meet up with a gossip blogger who goes by the moniker Perez Hilton. We were scheduled to make the scene at an MTV party in some majestic French château, but when I met up with Perez in front of a beachside casino, he informed me that the plan had changed: it turned out Paris was having a private dinner party and Perez was way tight with his nom de plume-sake. Before you could say, "That's hot," we were at the restaurant Baoli and I was sitting right next to the world's most famous devisee.

I can confirm that Paris uses her famous catchphrase with regularity in casual conversation and that it just gets funnier and funnier each time you hear it. I'm telling you, of all the craziness I experienced in Cannes—hell, damn near anywhere I've ever been—spending five hours in close company with Paris and Perez Hilton ranks among the most surreal. We sipped mojitos from the same glass and drank specialty bottles of 1996 Dom Pérignon* the size of Mini-Me (no exaggeration). After a meal that must have cost more than a presidential campaign, we headed into the nightclub section of Baoli, where Paris got up and sang a cover of Rod Stewart's "Do Ya Think I'm Sexy." I'm pretty sure she winked at me during the chorus, too, and at that moment I instantly regretted every negative word I'd ever written about her. I decided right then and there that I wouldn't make any snarky comments about her vocal stylings, either: I'd let her CD warble for itself.

The primary directive I had been given for composing a daily journal at Cannes was simple enough: give readers who aren't very familiar with the film festival a sense of what it *feels* like to be there. Okay, so try to imagine you've had a very long day in which you've been

---

* The 1996 vintage is legendary. Vintage wines generally are released five years after harvest, but the rule of thumb is that they don't come into their own until they've aged eight to ten years. Readers who have a handle on basic math will note that the '96 is now at the front end of maturity.

shoved around by aggressive reporters, rude paparazzi, and overzealous fans from the four corners of the globe, while also absorbing a tremendous amount of guff from haughty publicists and ill-tempered security guards. Some time around midnight you venture out into the warm presummer's evening in search of a comfortable watering hole for the purpose of getting pissed, and after walking for what seems like miles you stumble upon Morrison's, an honest-to-goodness Irish pub smack dab in the heart of Cannes on the Rue Teisseire. Why settle on a working-class Irish joint when you're in one of the ritziest resort towns on the French Riviera in the midst of the world's most celebrated film festival? That's easy: for a variety of reasons, some of them partially valid—you're intimidated by people from other countries (i.e., France, Venezuela, China) and other planets (i.e., Hollywood).

Are you *feeling* Cannes yet?

"This is the oldest, biggest, busiest, and best-run Irish establishment in town," averred Morrison's barkeep Robert Ryan, who calls Limerick home, adding: "Don't put that down, though—the cops might find me." I mentioned that my own Irish lineage stems from Cork County, whereupon Ryan quipped, "Sorry to hear that." He told me that Morrison's ownership group had purchased the space next door and that the already roomy bar would be expanded in time for the following year's festival. "It won't be double the fun, it'll be double the abuse," he cackled, baring a twisted grin that suggested he wasn't kidding. It was ALL GOOD, though, because unlike the publicists and security guards at Cannes, the Irish bartenders there at least have the decency to serve your derision with a delicious Guinness chaser or two. . . . *Slainte!*

In Cannes there were hordes of fans gathered each day outside the Palais de Festival in hopes of seeing movie stars, and to call these folks devoted is like calling Robert Novak a nasty old hack . . . it just doesn't quite cover the bill. Birgitte Yager was a twenty-four-year-old from Denmark, and while I'm no geologist, I'm pretty sure that's pretty far from Cannes. Birgitte had traveled to Cannes on holiday with a girl-friend and claimed to have spent the majority of her time camped out at the Palais, camera in hand, trying to get close to the stars. She wasn't kidding, either, because when we met it was the middle of the after-noon on a gorgeous beach day many hours before the next red-carpet event. She should have been tanning, but instead she was "fanning." Damn shame, too, because Birgitte had it going on and the beaches in Cannes are top-optional.

"Maybe this afternoon someone famous comes to visit the press," she said, explaining her dubious strategy. I had to suppress a giggle— can you imagine Tom Hanks popping into the cramped media room for a spell? Birgitte had already "got" Hanks, and proudly showed off a digital image of him she'd snapped on the red carpet days earlier at *The Da Vinci Code* world premiere. She said she "loved" Hanks but hadn't seen the movie yet. I didn't have the heart to tell her it blows. Her wish list also included Ethan Hawke (he'd been in Cannes to promote *Fast Food Nation*), Greg Kinnear (ditto), Penelope Cruz (*Volver*), The Rock (*Southland Tales*), and Brad Pitt, who starred in *Babel* but wasn't scheduled to be there for its premiere. When I told her as much, Birgitte didn't miss a beat: "Perhaps he comes to see you, the press." Uh, yeah.

While in Cannes I finally discovered a liquor company that truly *gets* me. Leblon makes cachaça, and although I've never actually tasted it, I'd like to go on record as saying it is my favorite cachaça in the world. Okay, I'm kidding. I actually drank gallons of Leblon in the South of France but the cachaça isn't what sold me on the company—their hospitality did. Throughout the festival Leblon made personal assistants available—gratis—to filmmakers, stars, and, yes, even lowly journalists like *moi*. According to Tracy Gilbert, who was Leblon's VP of global marketing, offering personal assistants to the press was in no way a gimmick designed to garner favorable coverage, but rather a way of "letting our friends in the media know that we understand how stressful it can be working a huge festival such as Cannes, and that we'd like to help." I appreciated that level of altruism . . . almost as much as all the free booze, VIP party passes, and T-shirts Leblon had given me. Hey, the stars clean up on swag—what's wrong with the Little People getting a little, too? And sure, so maybe Leblon ultimately winds up getting seriously favorable ink in a national best seller,* but it's not like they *planned* it that way. Seriously! Ask Tracy Gilbert if you don't believe me.

My assistant was Sophie Kristelle Jacq, a lovely woman from Cannes who divided her time living there and in St. Barts. You gotta love the French Riviera, eh? Even the assistants live the high life! First thing every morning I had Sophie dump a pitcher of cold water on my head because the night before had invariably been a rough one. Then I'd instruct her to hit the main drag, La Croissette, to do some "person on the street" interviews while I went back to bed for a few hours. I'd

---

* *Nobody Likes a Quitter (and other reasons to avoid rehab)* by Dan Dunn

also have Sophie go off and review the movies I was supposed to be seeing, a number of which she told me I enjoyed very much. She had other duties, too. You know, mundane stuff such as some much-needed eyebrow tweezing, calling my friends in the States to let them know that I was having a lot more fun than they were, and of course taking column dictation and translating my screeds into seven different languages . . . just in case.

Perhaps the most unsettling development at the 59th Festival de Cannes was the return of that most heinous of Reagan-era fashion transgressions: the khaki shorts/polo-shirt-with-sweater-knotted-around-the-neck ensemble. According to one of my colleagues from *Metro*'s Paris office, this particular attire atrocity was *très branché* among the French upper crust, who were out in full force on the Riviera looking very much like Robert Wagner circa his *Hart to Hart* heyday. It was an inauspicious occurrence, indeed, that augured the inevitable comeback of the tragic parachute pants/"Chams" muscle shirt combo that, as many fashionistas may recall, torpedoed poor Danny Terio's career.

Among the enduring memories of my two weeks at the 2006 Festival de Cannes were lively conversations with movie stars such as Cillian Murphy, Keanu Reeves, Robert Downey Jr., and Sam Jackson, seeing *Borat* and *Babel* for the first time, checking into Paris Hilton, as well as the night I was nearly run down by a vehicle carrying supermodel Eva Herzigova. And how could I forget all the amazing parties? Well, that's easy: Leblon* and its potent memory-sapping properties.

---

* Yes, it's another shameless plug!

I met all sorts of fascinating individuals who lurked behind the scenes, too: producers, publicists, managers, journalists, festival staff, security guards, and, of course, the street vendors around the fest's headquarters who sold the relatively affordable sandwiches and snacks that I subsisted on day in and day out . . . the shit wasn't too nasty, but it'll be a while before I go back on the all-ham-and-cheese-panini diet again.

When it really comes down to it, though, the Cannes encounter that has surely been etched into my memory forever took place with a lovely young Parisian woman upon whom I was, as they say in that country, "putting the moves." Although she spoke very little English, we managed to communicate fairly well, and she understood when I extended an offer to visit me in the States sometime on holiday. "Okay," she said, flashing a smile bright enough to blind whatever the opposite of a bat is, "I come on you in America." Mon amour, I couldn't have said it better myself.

⋅ ♈ 🏆 ♈ ⋅

Earlier in this tome I denounced the mixing of spirits such as vodka with Red Bull and other energy drinks. After all, alcohol is a depressant; Red Bull's a stimulant. They're at opposite ends of the body's functional spectrum, and I reckoned that bringing them together could be as precarious as when they mixed matter and antimatter on *Star Trek*. But at the 2007 Sundance Film Festival I began to reconsider my position. I spent seven days and nights embedded inside the watering holes of Park City, Utah, for the purpose of studying the alcohol-intake patterns of celebrities, and during that time it became increasingly evident that vodka and Red Bull has serious sex appeal.

To wit: at a party sponsored by *Hollywood Life* magazine, I found myself at the bar—what else is new, right?—standing next to actor Jeremy Sisto. Now, it may have been the altitude or, ahem, a burgeoning man-crush, but when Sisto ordered a vodka and Red Bull— DIET Red Bull, no less—instead of rolling my eyes and/or making a sarcastic remark as I usually do, I inexplicably found myself telling the bartender, "I'll have one of those, too." What can I say? I was a big *Six Feet Under* fan.

After we got our drinks, Jeremy joked about watching his figure and I laughed, probably a little too loudly. A group of very pretty women was standing nearby smiling at us. So I raised my vodka and diet Red Bull in a mock toast to them, and they giggled and waved. I turned back toward Jeremy, as I desperately wanted the ladies to think he was my friend, but he was gone. So, too, I figured, was any chance I had at a love connection. But to my surprise the cutest of the bunch, a comely brunette named Ashley, came up to me and asked what I was drinking.

"That's my favorite," she cooed.

"Mine, too!" I lied. "My buddy Jeremy Sisto likes them, too."

"Who's that?" she asked.

"Nobody," I replied, jiggling the ice in my glass. "Let's try the green Red Bull on the next round."

Step 10

What Would Jesus Drink? A Holiday Hootch Guide

"It's a righteous thing to do, man . . . it's like spiked eggnog for the soul."

And so it was that Bottomfeeder had convinced me to join him and his band of merry degenerates—the Unacceptable Behavior Club (UBC)—on yet another rowdy misadventure: going door-to-door singing Christmas carols while intoxicated. Very, very intoxicated. Think "Tommy Lee on his birthday"–type tanked. It was a move of professional survival. Perhaps somebody out there still thinks that *Saturday Night Live* is funny, but it sure isn't anyone with a modicum of taste.* But on a Saturday night just before Jesus's 2,006th birthday, stopping home for a fresh shirt after yet another shots-fest disaster, there were Bottomfeeder and the UBC, watching *SNL* with the sort of intensity usually reserved for porn downloads or double overtime.

---

* That hilarious "Dick in a Box" sketch with Justin Timberlake being the only notable exception in the past five years.

"Genius," one of them muttered as some lame premise went poorly executed. "Makes me feel like singing Christmas carols."

Then came, "It's a righteous thing to do, man . . . it's like **spiked eggnog for the soul.**" Given that I'd had too much spiked eggnog already, I was in no mood to argue. Someone handed me a Santa hat, and I slid it over my dome. Our first order of business (after topping off plastic bourbon flasks) was to generate some sort of set list—no easy task given Bottomfeeder's oddly intense aversion to traditional holiday numbers.

The Candy Cane Martini

2 1/2 parts Stolichnaya vodka
1/2 part peppermint schnapps (Hiram Walker is my suggestion)
1/2 part crème de cacao
candy cane to garnish

Pour Stoli and schnapps in a shaker with shaved ice. Shake well and strain into a martini glass. Hook the candy cane over the side to garnish.

"How about 'Deck the Halls'? That's a good one," said Sully, the UBC's longest tenured member, sergeant-at-arms, and the only man I know who lists multiple rehab "graduations" on his résumé.

"Nah. I don't get it," Bottomfeeder snorted. "I mean, what are 'boughs of holly,' anyways? Besides, the stuff about donning gay apparel makes me uncomfortable."

Sully suggested changing the words to something a bit more UBC-esque.

"Sure, like, 'Now let's put on our "I'm With Stupid" T-shirts . . . fa-la-la-la-la-la-la-la-la!!!'" sang Bottomfeeder. I found that very disconcerting considering that I was, in fact, with stupid. Several stupids, actually. The UBC, however, all got a good laugh out of Bottomfeeder.

"I don't know if you can just go ahead and defile the words to 'Deck the Halls,'" I argued. "I mean, we're talking about a timeless holiday classic here."

"Look, man," he replied, "we're not defiling—just sampling. This is the Modern World, where running old ladies off the highway to increase traffic flow is considered a public service. Tradition is the stuff landfills are made of." But after several disastrous attempts to rhyme "yuletide" with a type of lewd sex act, the UBC was forced to change its tune.

"Rock stars do some cool Christmas songs," muttered Tubby Joe, a large red-faced Irishman given to wearing Notre Dame T-shirts. "How 'bout we try one of those?"

"Does Black Sabbath have one?" Sully wondered aloud.

"No," said Joe, "but Billy Squire does."

Everyone agreed that Billy Squire did have a hell of a Christmas rocker in his repertoire, but because not one of us could remember a single verse, it was decided (with me dissenting) that any Billy Squire song would suffice. So it was that we wound up on a neighbor's porch a short time later, alternately belting out the choruses to "The Stroke" and "My Kinda Lover." Two doors down, Sully mentioned something about a John Lennon yuletide carol, and before you knew it we were warbling "Instant Karma" at the top of our lungs.

"Doesn't caroling make you feel like an erect nipple?" Bottomfeeder effused as he surveyed the Blackberry he'd just lifted from underneath someone's tree. Since losing that plum role to David Faustino, my roomie's career had gone colder than Osama Bin Laden's trail.* This was the happiest I'd seen him in weeks.

"Nope," I responded, struggling to remain upright under the weight of an empty flask of bourbon. "I'm beginning to feel like I'm part of a bad *SNL* skit."

"Funny you should mention that," said Bottomfeeder, "cuz later on we gotta meet up with Jimmy Fallon and some of his people and . . ." He began ticking off a list of names of past and present *SNL* cast members, but I'd already given myself over to the benumbing virtues of eggnog and bourbon and would soon be down for the count.

I can't recall when, exactly, but something *did* happen over the last holiday season. I had what philosophers and 12-step counselors refer to as a Profound Realization . . . an Xmas afflatus, if you will. It occurred to me that unlike most everything else here in this City of Angels—this deeply flawed yet intoxicatingly effervescent convolution I call home—Christmas Spirit is not something tangible, something you can buy at Fred Segal or order off the dinner menu at Spago. Christmas Spirit is powerful but ephemeral, not at all unlike when an infant passes one of their little gas bombs; you either pick up the unmistakable, overwhelming scent—"Aren't you a stinky little cutie?"—or it just slips right under your nose without your ever having caught the slightest whiff.

---

* I sincerely hope that by the time this tome makes it into print, the evildoing Al Qaeda leader will have been captured and brought to justice, rendering this particular metaphor inapplicable. I'm also pulling for the Kansas City Royals to win the World Series.

On the morning after the UBC caroling adventure the only thing I was smelling was the mephitic odor of stale beer, cigarettes, and other virulent vapors indigenous to the small, grubby one-bedroom apartment I'm forced to share with my roommate, one Mr. Bottomfeeder. There were no Christmas tunes playing when I awoke, hungover and sprawled naked on the floor, surrounded by empty bottles and half-smoked butts. Instead, thanks to the infernal Continuous Loop feature on the CD player, I was greeted by some screaming no-talent trying to squeeze the last drop of blood from the lifeless corpse that was once the Seattle Sound. Call it the Grunge Who Stole Christmas.

Talk about devastation. Just a few days 'til December 25, and I was stuck in a filthy hole-in-the-wall apartment on the opposite coast from my family and loved ones, listening to an Alice in Chains cover band and reeking like something Bottomfeeder had dragged in.* To make matters worse, the thing he had dragged in—some junkie he'd met underneath the Santa Monica Pier—was lying in a puddle of her own vomit . . . in my bed. I remember thinking, *This is no way to spend the holidays, no matter how much I deserve it.* Next thing I knew, I was roaming the streets, nose tilted to the heavens, hoping beyond hope to pick up the vapor trail of Christmas Spirit.

---

* When police discovered the corpse of Alice in Chains singer Layne Staley in his Seattle apartment in 2002, he'd been dead for nearly two weeks. Staley probably didn't smell very pleasant, either.

⚡ This One's for You, Bob ⚡

A few weeks before Christmas 2006, several friends and I had traveled to Honolulu to see Pearl Jam open for U2 on the final stop of the latter band's *Vertigo* world tour. It was an electric, emotionally charged concert with an unforgettable encore that featured both acts in a rousing cover of Neil Young's "Keep on Rockin' (in the Free World)." Outstanding as it was, however, the concert isn't my most cherished memory of our time in Oahu. Not by a long shot. Not after the day we spent with Bob Addobati. He isn't a famous musician, but at eighty-four years young Bob was by far the biggest star we encountered in Hawaii, and a big reason why there's still a free world for any of us to rock in. Bob is one of very few remaining survivors of the Japanese attack on Pearl Harbor in 1941. He wasn't injured on that fateful day, although he lost his leg four years later in a torpedo attack while serving in the Pacific. After they fitted him with a prosthetic, he gave his country seven more years of service.

We met Bob and his daughters by the pool at our Waikiki Beach hotel, and before we could gleefully shout, "booze cruise," the robust ole navy man was seabound with us aboard a catamaran sipping one-dollar Mai Tais and admiring what he politely referred to as the "lovely tomatoes." For decades, Bob had been returning to Pearl Harbor to attend an official ceremony every fifth December, but this trip was to be his last. Bob said he realized that even a "tough, one-legged SOB" like him could not withstand the inexorable march of time. "Who knows how many of us, if any, will be left five years from now?" he wondered aloud. Shortly before we parted ways, Bob patted me on the back and told me that spending the day with us had been "a real gift." Indeed it was—the best I've received in many years. For that, for everything, Bob, I thank you. We all do. *Mahalo!*

It was nowhere to be found at the liquor store, but I did procure a bottle of Baileys Original Irish Cream, the perfect holiday libation. I was damned determined to sniff out some undistilled Christmas Spirit, but I figured it would be wise to have a little something extra on hand to help put out any emotional fires . . . you know, should my quest take a turn for the worse. Next stop was the Record Cellar, where I bartered a few sips of Baileys for a used copy of *Elvis' Christmas*

*Album.** Now it goes without saying that there has never been, nor will there ever be, a finer Christmas crooner than the King (with all apologies to Nat King Cole). And you can kiss my ass with that Bing Crosby crap! Elvis is the real deal. Could Bing Crosby have died on the shitter and still remained a bad mofo like E? I don't think so. So I popped in the CD and for an hour or so I was transported to a happier, more yuletide-friendly place. And right then I knew that in order to find and maintain the TRUE Christmas Spirit, I would have to inspire others with song, the way Elvis had inspired me. I had to go Christmas caroling again, and I had to do it right! I enlisted Bottomfeeder, who, despite his expansive list of shortcomings, possessed two things I did not: a guitar and the ability to carry a tune. I know, I know! Wonders will never cease.

Bottomfeeder and I set out into the unusually cold night with a song in our collective heart and the rest of the Baileys in my bag. We swung by O'Brien's pub, where, after a few glasses of fortified eggnog and a brief argument over whether or not to include the Bing Crosby parts, we delivered a rousing rendition of "The Little Drummer Boy." Many of the bar patrons were visibly moved. So was Bottomfeeder. Without warning, he launched into "All the Young Dudes" by Mott the Hoople. Christmas fare it ain't, but dammit if we didn't rock the house something proper.

Things didn't go as smoothly caroling door-to-door. In fact, several people threatened to shoot us with automatic weapons. And as if that weren't hairy enough, it got so damn cold down by the beach that Bottomfeeder's hand froze to the neck of his guitar and my lips congealed

---

* "Silent Night" is guaranteed to melt your heart, but you can fix that with a little chilled Sambuca.

to my teeth. Consequently, for most of the evening I was forced to mumble every song in G. But we persevered. We played houses, bars, and restaurants. At one point, we had nearly two dozen people on the Third Street Promenade singing along to the all-G version of the Pretenders' "2,000 Miles." We were boozed-up buskers making merry, and the feeling was sweeter than the smell of chestnuts roasting on an open fire or the sound of herald angels singing. It was later, outside a 7-11, just after a particularly rousing performance of the Kinks' "Father Christmas," that I had a seriously out-of-body Christmas experience.

A strong wind suddenly blew in carrying a strange silvery dust that caused everyone standing around to sneeze uncontrollably for nearly two minutes. When the snorting and wheezing finally died down, a little handicapped boy named Tiny Tom miraculously leapt from his wheelchair and shouted, "God bless you, all of you," and started handing out Kleenex. Bottomfeeder and I knew we'd just witnessed a Christmas miracle. We hoisted Tiny Tom up on our shoulders and ran through the streets of Santa Monica, caroling at the top of our lungs—simply having a wonderful Christmas time. A short while later we were picked up by the cops. After some serious explaining, Tom's parents agreed to drop all charges. They even let us sing the little guy a farewell song, Run DMC's "Christmas in Hollis."

Then I was walking home, and the night seemed slightly unreal. *Had it all been a dream?* I stopped near a cliff and gazed out to the sea, blanketed as it was by a big, starry sky. *These are indeed Strange Days, but I'm alive, life is beautiful, and it's Christmas time.* The chill left my body and I felt more peaceful than I had in a very long time. I tilted my head back, breathed in the night air, and smiled, expecting to smell the ocean or perhaps smoke from a nearby chimney. Instead my nostrils detected something totally unexpected—something wonderful. . . .

I smelled baby farts.

. ♈ ♉ ♈ .

Not that long ago I came across an interesting report in *Esquire* about a professor at Carnegie Mellon University who has developed a set of goggles that translate speech in real time. I imagine a device like that might be useful in a nightclub—say around 1:00 AM, an hour when female patrons often say things to men that we can't understand, such as, "No, I will not go home with you," "Get that mistletoe away from me," and, "Beat it, loser." Yep, I bet a set of those goggles sure would make for an excellent Christmas gift, but then again, what do I know? Hell, it cracks me up whenever readers of my column write in to request holiday buying tips because, while I certainly have my finger on the pulse of the wine and spirits industry, when it comes to conventional "gifting" I'm all thumbs. Last Christmas, for instance, I gave my sister Gatorade. My brother got firewood. Mom said she loved her new FUBU rugby shirt, but I'm pretty sure she was just being gracious. My then-girlfriend, on the other hand, made little effort to hide her disappointment in our weekend getaway for six (me, her, and four of my buddies) to the world-famous EMR Paintball Park in New Milford, Pennsylvania. I learned my lesson, though—next time I take a gal to play paintball I'm going to let her win at least one round. And from now on, everyone on my list is getting booze for Christmas.

I've always enjoyed making lists. As a child I'd spend hours alone in my room with a journal meticulously recording my preferred bands, movies, and sports stars, just to name a few. As I grew older, lonelier, and, shall we say, more lugubrious, I'd often enumerate such things as favorite natural disasters, most despised historic figures, and hideous afflictions matched with people I wished suffered from them. Eventually my parents got me on medication, and most of the "dark stuff" went away. But my fondness for lists and pills endures to this day, one of the many reasons why I love being a journalist at Christmas, the most list-crazy time of the year. In fact, I just popped a few Xanax, made my Christmas shopping list, and checked it thrice to one-up that fat bastard Santa. I hope that some of you will find the following suggestions useful. Those who do not, well, you can ho-ho-blow-me and/or skip ahead to Step 11. My editor has insisted that I pad the pages of this book with some practical information about alcohol and seeing that we're, oh, about five-sixths of the way through, I'd best be getting around to it. Okay, then, a boozy holiday gift list:

DaVinci 2004 Chianti Classico ($24)—You don't have to be a code-breaking symbologist with a bad hairdo to get to the bottom of this bottle. A well-balanced red with a spicy finish that pairs well with osso bucco or cheese ravioli. Ideal for an Italian-style Christmas celebration.

Riedel's "O" Martini Glass ($25 per set of two)—Part of the esteemed designer's stemless collection, the "O" glass's classic bowl sits atop a grooved and hollowed base. It's elegantly modern . . . just like me and you! Best thing is, "O" is half the price of the Riedel Vinum glass it's modeled after. And who doesn't love a good Vinum glass at Christmas, eh? (Definition of Vinum not included.)

ϟ Our Spirits Survey Says . . . ϟ

The Christmas season officially begins at Thanksgiving, a tradition dating back to the early seventeenth century when the Pilgrims celebrated a successful harvest by inviting their Native American neighbors over for supper, then massacring them and stealing their land. In the spirit of "give and take" passed down by our ancestors, I'm GIVING some friends an opportunity to share the most important lessons they've learned about the Drinking Life, while TAKING a respite from the grind of serious spirits reportage. My best advice to you, friends, is to beware the freakin' Pilgrims—they're ruthless SOBs, especially after they've been boozing. Here are some other nuggets of wino wisdom:

"Bright blue is not a color that should ever appear in your glass after you've passed the age of six."

—Terry Sullivan, contributing editor, *The Malt Advocate*

(What this world needs is more tolerance and understanding—just ask the Native Americans—so with that in mind, this Christmas Terry will be receiving a bottle of Hypnotiq, a mixture of vodka, cognac, and fruit juices that is as blue as the holiday season is long.)

"How is it that you can sue a cigarette company for cancer & McDonald's for getting fat, but u cant sue BUDWEISER 4 all the UGLY people u f—-?" Hahahah!! This is what I have learned!!!"

—Tommy Lee, drummer, Mötley Crüe

(It should be noted that Tommy e-mailed this gem to me at four o'clock in the morning on a Monday. For being a good sport, he'll receive a case of Pilsner Urquell, the venerable brew from the Czech Republic that is clinically proven to reduce the risk of beer goggles.)

"The bathrooms are always farther away than you think."

—Curtis Robinson, Crisis Manager to the Stars

(Curtis will surely enjoy his new "Stadium Pal," a male catheter worn just like a condom in which pee is passed through a plastic hose and collected into a plastic bag strapped to the leg. We've come a long way since the seventeenth century, eh?)

"I'm on the Thirteenth Step of a Twelve-Step Program. Now I know why I drink, and I agree, I should be drinking."

—Jackie "The Jokeman" Martling

(I should point out that Jackie quit drinking years ago. Good thing he hasn't stopped being funny.)

Champagne Krug Grande Cuvée MV ($145)—This bubbly is, quite simply, unforgettable. If I were being exiled to the proverbial desert island and could bring only five bottles of champagne (NO WAY I'm narrowing it down further), this one makes the cut. I'd also bring a bucket with ice . . . to the island, that is.

Toña Cerveza ($7.99 per six-pack)—Give the beer lover in your life the first-ever Nicaraguan import widely available in the United States. This lager-style brew is named after a sexy Latina girl (is there any other kind?) and packs a wallop at 4.6 percent alcohol by volume.

St. Supéry Virtú 2002 White Meritage ($30)—I flipped (and subsequently injured my back) over this dynamic wine from Napa. It's a blend of Sauvignon Blanc and Sémillon grapes harvested at night to maintain their ripe fruit flavor, because staleness, apparently, is afraid of the dark.

Ardbeg "Airigh Nam Beist" ($115)—"Airigh Nam Beist" (pronounced "arry-nam-baysht"), or "the Beast," as it's known in some circles, is the new premium expression of Ardbeg, a lesser-known whisky in the U.S. market that is utterly revered throughout Scotland.

DH Krahn gin ($27)—Krahn is citrusy and dry, with heavy juniper notes that blossom in the finish. Distilled in Stupfler Alambic pot stills, the so-called "Rolls Royce" of copper Alambics. Tastes great with Schweppes, the "bitchin' Camaro" of tonics.

The Luxury Spirits of the Month Club ($1,000)—The lucky recipient of this high-end gift will receive a different bottle of premium hootch each month for an entire year. We're talking Johnnie Walker Blue in January, Bulleit Bourbon in May, and Clynelish 14-Year-Old

Whisky in November, to name a few. Beats the hell outta Gatorade, don't it? (Purchase at www.luxurybar.com.)

Absente ($35 per 750 ml bottle)—Absinthe liqueur was banned in America in 1915 because it contained thujone, the hallucinogenic component in wormwood plants. This was unfortunate news for all the writers, poets, and painters who nipped absinthe to stoke their creative fires, but a victory for militant prohibitionists convinced that any liquid that made people feel exceptionally chill must be Devil's brew. Today, a similar strain of zealot is running this country and, as you might expect, thujone—which admittedly sounds like something a dangerous foreigner might try to sneak onto a plane—is still illegal. Absente is a 110-proof modern version of the infamous green hootch that contains "southern wormwood," regular ole wormwood's less bitter, less thujone-y cousin. Is it a mere coincidence that President Bush pretends to be from the South and that southern wormwood is legal? Probably, yeah. But let the conspiracy theories roll anyway. Hell, slug some Absente to stimulate the paranoid synapses while you're working it all out. Here's how to prepare it: Place a sugar cube on a slotted spoon and hold it over a glass containing three ounces of Absente. Slowly drip three ounces of cold water over the sugar to dissolve it. Watch the Absente change color to an opalescent green. Drink . . . and away you go!

A Barrel of Jack Daniel's ($9,000)—If one bottle of whiskey just won't cut it, how about 240? That's how much hootch fills an entire barrel of Jack Daniel's Single Barrel Tennessee Whiskey. For roughly the cost of a Hyundai or a big night in Vegas, you get the bottled whiskey, the empty barrel in which it was aged, a brass plaque, and a framed certificate of ownership.

ZEN Green Tea Liqueur ($30)—While this isn't my cup of for-tified green tea, Bottomfeeder went gaga for the stuff in a chilled shot called Zen Shui. It's made with an ounce each of gin and ZEN with a dash of fresh lime juice . . . Persian limes if you can get 'em.

Trump Vodka ($40)—It's no secret that the Donald likes to slap his name on phallic symbols and that there are only so many towers out there for the branding. Still, the guy claims to have never even tasted coffee let alone more intoxicating legal stimulants, so Trump peddling vodka seems as unlikely as Mel Gibson backing a line of designer yarmulkes. At the time of the brand's 2006 launch, the Toupeed Tycoon himself went on Don Imus's syndicated radio show to explain his decision, saying, "I know it's like tobacco companies making cigarettes and then advertising 'don't smoke,' which I think is ridiculous," adding, "but it's a legal product and if I don't sell it someone else will." Ah, I see—so he's just trying to beat Ivanka and Donald Jr. to the punch. The people the King of Self-Glorification hired to promote his brand have dubbed Trump Vodka "The World's Finest Super Premium Vodka," and while the folks at Ketel One and Grey Goose, among others, would certainly beg to differ, it says here that Trump is a well-rounded, competitively priced spirit. Esteemed master craftsman Jacques de Lat of Wanders Distillery, which has been producing vodka since 1631, makes Trump in Holland. It then goes into a distinctive bottle designed by famed artist Milton Glaser. And while DT was a bit off the mark in predicting that, "By the summer of oh-six, I fully expect the most called-for cocktail in America to be the 'T&T,' or the 'Trump and Tonic,'" history suggests one should never bet against this guy.

Reyka Vodka ($23)—Reyka comes from Iceland; so does Björk. I dig Björk, so I tried Reyka. It's good vodka. Not the Sugarcubes' *Life's Too Good* good, but a damn sight better than Björk's soundtrack for "Dancer in the Dark."

Caravella Limoncello ($17)—Wanna get away? Turn up the heat in your apartment, squeeze into your bathing suit, slather on some Hawaiian Tropic, and serve the limoncello with unsweetened iced tea in a tall glass over ice. Add sugar to taste. Think summer.

Step 11

I'm Only Hanging On to Watch You Go Down

When the Beast's hired goons arrived at my door, I had an inkling that they hadn't come bearing good tidings. Large men with low IQs in the employ of unscrupulous attorneys seldom do. Fortunately, the cretins hadn't come to stomp my head in. One of them handed me a manila envelope while his associate documented the exchange with a video camera. Then, without saying a word, they left.

The envelope contained a note from the Beast demanding that I "cease and desist with any and all creative endeavors related to the personal life of my client." The client he referred to was the unkempt, unemployed, unoustable slug who at that very moment was sprawled out on my sofa, wearing what had been my favorite pair of boxer shorts, and watching—for the sixth time in half as many days—a DVD copy of *Team America: World Police*.

"Relax," Bottomfeeder said matter-of-factly as I wrestled with a nearly irresistible urge to throttle him once and for all. "The letter's just a formality. You can keep writing about me in your little book thingy so long as a few conditions are met."

"Conditions?" I growled.

"Yeah. Just a couple of deal points. No biggie," he replied, his eyes shifting back to the movie. "Oh, this is the part where the puppets get it on. It's the best!"

That's when I blew my top. I'm pretty sure my bottom dropped out, too.

"What *conditions*, man?!" I hollered. "What the fuck more could you possibly want from me?!!!"

"Whoa—easy there, big man. There's no reason to go ballistic," Bottomfeeder said. "In fact, you should be thrilled. You see, I want to play *you* in my next movie."

As is so often the case when it comes to the utterings of my bloodsucking boarder, I didn't see that one coming.

"Me?"

"Yes, YOU!" he replied. "Or at least a character based on you."

Against my better judgment, I was intrigued. "Really? Me? A movie? Wow! What's it about?"

Bottomfeeder paused the DVD, sat up, and cleared his throat.* Obviously he was serious about this movie idea of his, and since the project potentially involved me and some form of financial remuneration, I tried my damnedest to overlook his being shrouded in nothing but underwear and the stench of whiskey combined with God knows what else while watching puppets give each other golden showers.

"Well," he said, shifting into on-the-lot pitch-meeting mode. "Think *Barfly* meets *The Bourne Identity*."

---

* Imagine the sound an old garbage disposal makes, only significantly less sonorous.

Admittedly, I had a difficult time marrying two such divergent concepts. Then again, far crazier ideas were bandied about in Hollywood every day.*

"At first, this guy seems like just another down-on-his-luck hack writer—he drinks too much, always rambling on about stuff nobody gives a shit about; a complete fuck-up with the ladies, flat broke . . . you know what I'm talking about."

"And this guy's based on me?" I asked, as my enthusiasm took a sudden nosedive into an empty pool of disillusionment.

"Exactly," he said. "But unlike you, this guy's not who he *appears* to be." Then he leaned in close and lowered his voice. "The writing gig is just a cover, see? He's CIA, antiterrorism division, tracking Islamic fundamentalists who want to blow up America."

I checked my enthusiasm for signs of life. There was still a pulse. So I inquired, "You mean he's only *pretending* to be a loser, when in reality he's a dashing spy who saves millions of lives?"

"No!" Bottomfeeder replied.

"No?" I asked.

"There's a twist."

"But I thought his being a CIA agent instead of a writer *was* the twist," I said.

"Yeah, that's the *first* twist," Bottomfeeder explained, "but these days you've got to have two twists . . . minimum."

"O-kay," I said warily. "What's the second twist?"

"Our guy's a traitor who is actually working *for* the Islamic

---

* You can keep your Yanomamö Indian jokes to yourself, thank you very much.

terrorists. He's planted dirty bombs in every major U.S. city and plans to detonate them on Christmas morning."

"So let me get this straight," I said. "Instead of redeeming himself by saving the country from evildoers, this poor, drunken, sexually frustrated bullshit artist who is based on me turns out to be a ruthless mass murderer?"

"Yep!" he beamed. My enthusiasm was dead. He'd pulled the plug.

"Doesn't seem like a particularly heroic role for an actor, does it?" I posited.

"That's where the third twist comes into play," he countered.

"Oh, the third twist," said I. "And what, pray tell, is the *third* twist?"

"Just as this guy's about to blast the U.S. of A. back to the Stone Age, it suddenly dawns on him what a complete piece of shit he's been his entire life—try and picture him illuminated in this, like, really bad-ass otherworldly glow while he's having this profound realization. So then there's this montage in which he goes around the country and personally disarms every one of the bombs . . . dressed up like Santa, cuz it's Christmas. And then when he's done, he takes his own life to ensure that he'll never be able to hurt anyone ever again."

I groaned. "He kills himself to save the world from himself?"

"You got it! That way I get to play the villain *and* the hero," Bottomfeeder said. "It's total duality-of-man type shit. People love that. Plus, my new agent is trying to negotiate a double billing in order to increase my quote. What do you think?"

"Sounds awesome," I sighed, thinking better of expending the sort of energy it would take to muster the appropriate level of sarcasm.

Then there was a knock at the door.

"That must be them," Bottomfeeder said, getting up to answer it.

"Who?" I asked.

"My new agent and our producer," he replied. "I asked them to drop by with the deal memo." Bottomfeeder opened the door to reveal Fisher,* a middle-aged Chinese man in a green leisure suit named Fong, and a guy toting a video camera who looked as if he'd just stepped out of a '60s surf movie. Fisher was carrying a six-pack of Smirnoff Ice.

"There he is," Fisher said with loud, feigned enthusiasm as he made his way over to me. He shook my hand and lied, "I've been meaning to call you to talk about some stuff in the offing, buddy." I hadn't heard from him in months, since the Fox deal fell apart. "Have you met Mr. Fong?"

"No," I said, "but I'm familiar with his work," recalling an expensive white dress shirt I'd taken to Fong's dry-cleaning joint that had come back pink and missing several buttons.

Fisher handed me a Smirnoff Ice. "Are you getting this?" he said to the surf dude with the camera, who nodded and made a twirling gesture with his finger.

"Oh, right—could you turn the bottle around so the label is visible, please? Thanks," Fisher instructed me.

"Who's the guy with the camera?" I asked.

"That's Art," Fisher said. "He'll be documenting the making of the film from beginning to end."

---

* You *did* see that coming, right? Please, people, try to pay attention.

"The making of the film?" I asked incredulously. "So does that mean you've secured studio backing already?"

"Oh, there'll be no studios on this one. We're hoping to finance the entire film with money raised from liquor companies," Fisher gushed. "Product placement is where it's at these days."

Art waved at Fisher and made a "U-like" gesture with his finger.

"Dan, would you mind smiling a little more while you're holding the Smirnoff Ice?" Fisher said. "They gave us a little seed money."

Fong lit an unfiltered Pall Mall.

"Don't film that," Fisher told Art. "I'm trying to work a sponsorship deal with Marlboro."

"Look," I said, "I find it hard to believe that you're going to be able to line up enough liquor companies to fund something so ridiculous. A movie like this would cost at least fifty million. Have any of them seen the script?"

"There's no script yet," Fisher replied. "We haven't settled on a writer, but we've narrowed it down to two USC film school applicants."

"What about me?" I couldn't believe I found myself asking.

"I suggested you, of course," Fisher said, "but Smirnoff Ice wants someone a little more seasoned for this project. But, hey, I'm going to have you meet with them while you're in New York. If they like you, maybe we can score an associate producer's credit or something."

"New York?"

"You didn't tell him?" Fisher asked Bottomfeeder.

It turns out my space invader had had an idea about how he might best research the role of a sad-sack spirits scribe. He wanted to travel to New York City with me for a long weekend in which we would—as he put it—"play the press card" and abuse my position in the media in a most egregious manner.

"Call up some publicists and work your magic, man," he said. "We need luxury hotel suites, expensive bottles of booze, fancy dinners, and limousines. All comped, of course. We have to push this thing as far as we can and then some. My acting teacher says the purest expression of the art form can only be achieved through total immersion into character."

I told Bottomfeeder he was crazy if he honestly believed I'd jeopardize my career by calling in favors from publicists for *his* benefit. Hell, the away-from-home perks of my job were the only things left he'd yet to take from me.

With that, he pulled out his cell phone and started dialing.

"Who are you calling?" I asked.

"The Beast," Bottomfeeder shot back. "I'm gonna have him put the kibosh on that book of yours before it even has a chance to collect dust in the discount rack at Sam's Club."

So maybe it wasn't my proudest moment, but twenty-seven hours and fourteen calls to publicists later, Bottomfeeder and I—resplendent in our Smirnoff Ice sweatshirts—checked into a luxurious suite at the Dream Hotel in midtown Manhattan. From there, we made our way over to yet another fat room I'd secured at an Irish-themed hotel called the Fitzpatrick, where we left Art the surfer-documentarian. This would turn out to be an unwise decision on a number of levels, as it happened to be St. Patty's Day weekend and Art was of Celtic lineage, which, he would later tell hotel security, explained his lust for fermented beverages. He had a more difficult time, however, accounting for the impromptu "studio" he'd set up to videotape "auditions" for aspiring "leading ladies." Perhaps I could have done something to stop Art but alas, at the time of the alleged incident, I was busy unpacking a particularly fine array of single malts with Fong—who I'd gotten set up at the historic **Algonquin**—over at my *other* other room at the 70 Park Hotel on Thirty-eighth Street.

⚡ An Ode to Dorothy Parker ⚡

After a century in business, midnight comes easy to the Algonquin Hotel in midtown. Whenever I drop by to indulge in the quiet elegance of the place, my thoughts turn to the great spirits writer Dorothy Parker. It was, after all, Parker (not your crazy cousin) who invented the oft-used phrase, "I'd rather have a bottle in front of me than a frontal lobotomy." If she had a dime for every time somebody stole that zinger, she'd still be dead. But somebody would be rich. And I think she was writing about drink when she said, "Salary is no object. I want only enough to keep body and soul apart."

Ms. Parker and the hotel she helped make famous are more Makers Mark neat than bourbon and Coke; more martini than vodka soda. I gathered this information from someone who'd know—the head bartender at the Algonquin's Blue Bar, one Mr. Hoy who, at ninety years old and still pouring at this writing, is well versed in the classics.

It was wrong, all of it. My philandering ways had finally come full circle: sure, I'd been unfaithful to more than a few girlfriends in my time, but until that point I'd always been up-front with publicists. As I emptied the contents of the minibar at 70 Park, I remember experiencing something akin to acute stomach cramps. The feeling, a friend would later explain, was guilt. It's an inconvenient emotion, that one, although clearly not problematic enough to have induced me to curtail my bad behavior. Aw, hell, in my heart I'd always known the day would come when I'd drive the freebie train off the tracks—it's a predictable result in an industry set up so that some people are paid to give things away while others get paid to take them. In that regard spirits writing is just like taking part in politics or the People's Choice Awards.

Under the terms of the settlement, details regarding most of what went on that weekend cannot be included here. Besides, given the ridiculous amount of alcohol that was consumed, my memory of events is no better than a Bush administration official's at a congressional inquiry into the cause of . . . well, everything. I can tell you that one of the low points of our NYC excursion occurred shortly after I'd executed a perfect "freeloader flush" at the Dream Hotel. This move, familiar to anyone who's hosted a hospitality suite, is when you manage to get all your drunk friends, acquaintances, and hangers-on out of the room without any of them noticing that you, all the **free booze**, and the hottest chick at the party have stayed behind. Trust me, this is a complicated maneuver made all the more tricky when dealing with guests such as Bottomfeeder, who would rather shit thumbtacks than willingly abandon a room that is better stocked than the captain's chamber on Ted Kennedy's yacht. Fortunately, I'd had the foresight to arrange for an open tab at the White Horse Tavern and to start a rumor that DeNiro was over there drinking beneath the largest of that establishment's numerous paintings of Dylan Thomas. Indeed, Bottomfeeder et al. did not go gently into that good night. They went noisily, reciting memorable lines from *Raging Bull*.

❧ The Beverage Program for the Dream Suite Soiree ❧

Spirits:

Grand Marnier Cuvée du Centenaire

10 Cane Rum

Hennessy Cognac

Chopin Vodka

The Glenmorangie 'Sherry Cask Finish' Single Malt Scotch

Champagne/Sparkling Wine:

Veuve Clicquot La Grande Dame 1996

Dom Pérignon Vintage 1998

Taittinger Comtes de Champagne Rosé 1999

Dom Ruinart Blanc de Blanc

Domaine Carneros 'Le Rêve' 2000

Taittinger Comtes de Champagne Blanc de Blancs 1998

Wines:

Tenuta San Guido Sassicaia, Bolgheri Sassicaia DOC 2003

Tenuta San Guido Guidalberto 2004

Abadia Retuerta Pago Negralada 2002

Tenute del Cabreo 'Il Borgo' IGT 2003

Michele Chiarlo Barolo 'Cerequio,' DOCG 1999

Louis Jadot Bâtard-Montrachet, Grand Cru 2004

Bodegas RODA, RODA I 2002

Tenuta Sette Ponti 'Oreno' IGT 2004

Sequoia Grove Cabernet Sauvignon 'Rutherford Reserve' 2004

Wild Oak by St. Francis Chardonnay 2005

I remained at the Dream with a jaw-dropping dream named Ava, who had recently been "involved" with this guy Channing whom I sort of knew from the old Aspen days. In what I have to concede was an admirable bit of overachievement on the bet-hedging front, Channing had not only invited Ava to my suite party, he had brought along

another rod-busting beauty he'd been courting by the name of Tessa.
Allow me to make my case as I did during what's become known as
the "morning after 'man rules' powwow."

Let's say a friend . . . okay, someone you know* . . . asks you to take
what could be considered a trusted wingman position. Your mission
is to distract Girl A[†] while he pursues his interest in Girl B.[°]

"The question before the assembled is: did Dan betray the
wingman position?" Bottomfeeder posed as he sipped his third pre-
noon Smithwick's at the Pig 'n' Whistle at Third and Fifty-fifth. And
it must be noted that not since the day after the Hiroshima bombing
had a group of survivors looked as ragged as our lot did.

"No fucking way," I protested. Then I proceeded to build my case:
first off, Tessa . . . er, Girl B . . . A . . . whatever . . . Tessa, while an exem-
plary female specimen, was no Ava, five-time MVP of the League of
Her Own. This called Channing's man-judgment into question.
Second, I told him the moment he approached me with his duplici-
tous scheme that there was a definite vibe between Ava and me, thus
giving him every opportunity to lay down ground rules, reconsider his
options, or seek another wingman who didn't have the key to the
hotel suite along with a reputation for womanizing that was only
slightly more notable than that of Charlie Sheen.

"Sure, but it's quite a leap to go from running interference to

* In this case, Channing.

[†] Ava

[°] Tessa

having Ava alone in your hotel suite at two-thirty in the morning," Art interjected.

"Not really," I rejoindered, "because he left with Tessa and never came back!" I paused for a moment to let the implications of that dubious action sink in. Everyone knows that the statute of limitations for wingman loyalty is, at best, an hour in an "abandonment" situation . . . and even shorter when there's an open bar involved.

"Besides, all we did was talk," I continued, pounding the bar to punctuate the certitude with which I held my own innocence. "Yes, she wound up spending the night, but only because we fell asleep watching a movie. No bodily fluids were exchanged."

This raised everyone's eyebrows . . . including those of bar patrons we didn't know.

"You didn't even kiss her?" Fong gasped. It should be noted that whenever Fong opened his mouth to speak, which was a rare occurrence indeed, what came out invariably sounded like a gasp—the result of his having been a smoker since age seven.

"Nope," I attested.

"Why not?" Art asked.

"She said she only wanted to cuddle."

There was a collective groan. Most red-blooded males will tell you there's nothing worse than an attractive potential paramour who only wants to cuddle. It's like a perfect storm of frustration: she's inviting physical contact, which makes her seem willing or at least semi-gettable, while at the same time extinguishing any real hope you might have of putting Percy in the playpen on the first try.

"Please tell me you tried to use some cuddle-escalation techniques on her," a distressed Art begged, his tone a few octaves higher than normal.

"Didn't want to," I replied coolly. "Ava's different. I think I might love her."

The words hit them like a pie to the face—a lead pie, glass face. Imagine Hugh Hefner announcing he was going to date women his own age, Bill Maher swearing his allegiance to Karl Rove, or Raymond Teller* suddenly breaking into song. For a long moment, they all just sat there in stunned silence.

"I thought this day might never come again," Bottomfeeder announced finally. Then he gave me a hearty pat on the back. "Congratulations, my friend. If you're really, truly ready to love again, Ava is the right kind of woman to do it with."

"Yes," Fong concurred. "She total piece ass."

"Ava's an A-list Betty, that's for sure," Art nodded.

"But I'm still not convinced of your innocence vis-à-vis Channing," Bottomfeeder said. "After all, he had dibs on Ava, even if he did get temporarily waylaid chasing Tessa."

It was time for me to put my final piece of evidence into play—the bloody glove, if you will. I pulled out my Blackberry, called for quiet, and replayed the message Channing had left at 3:00 AM after he'd struck out with Tessa and discovered that Ava's ship had also sailed . . . with me battening down her hatches.

"Hey, Dan, it's Channing. . . . I just wanna make sure we're clear

---

* Penn's dance partner

about the shit you pulled with Ava. . . . Make sure you delete my number. . . . You're a total fucking two-timer. . . . Fuck you. . . . I wish I'd never met you."

The expressions on their faces said it all—the tribal shame hung in the air like the stench of post–St. Patty's Day vomit. Then again, it might have been the *actual* stench of post–St. Patty's Day vomit. Finally, someone mustered the strength to say what we'd all been thinking. . . .

"Delete my number? Two-timer? Wish I'd never met you?" Art repeated, taking a long, contemplative pull off his beer. "Holy shit! That dude went all *chick* on you!"

If they say "holy shit," you must acquit! My case, as they say, was rested. But the issue was far from settled. There was still serious mocking to be done.

"You know what you need to do," Bottomfeeder announced. "You need to *out-chick* him."

"Out-chick him?" I queried.

"Yes," he nodded. "Call him back and tell him that if he ever comes near you again you'll scratch his eyes out."

That cracked everyone up. Hell, even Fong was laughing.

Art added, "Then you need to text him and tell him that outfit he was wearing made him look fat."

Hooting and hollering all around. Then a random old guy at the end of the bar chimed in, "Tell him his shoes didn't match, either."

"Do shoe slams really piss them off, old-timer?" I yelled over to him.

"Why d'ya think I'm here instead of at home with my wife?" he replied.

⚲ 🏆 ⚲

The financing for the booze writer/terrorist film never did materialize. When the brass at Smirnoff Ice saw the grisly video Art shot in New York, they threatened to sue unless the footage was destroyed and their seed money returned with interest. After that, the best gig Fisher was able to land Bottomfeeder was fifth billing in a low-budget romantic comedy starring Steven Seagal. As for the poor kid Fisher had hired to pen the screenplay, he didn't get into USC film school, never saw a dime for the story outline he'd completed, and eventually was forced to take a job working the steam press at Fong's dry-cleaning shop. On the bright side, Fisher retained the kid as a client and even landed him a few gigs as an audience member.

I performed some damage control with the publicists before leaving New York, and upon my return to California did some soul searching. "Besotted" might be the best description for my condition throughout the weekend in the Big Apple, although witnesses have reported that I was "plastered," "lit," and "completely fuddled." My memories of the weekend's proceedings are foggier than the third act of *Cape Fear*, but I seem to recall an incident involving an overzealous bathroom attendant and some flying urinal cakes that led to my being forcibly removed from the lobby of yet another posh hotel. I lost my wallet sometime during that same evening, which explains why I wound up having such a hard time with that manager at the Taco Bell. And what does it say about our society when an upstanding member of the media like myself can't even be trusted to make good on a promise to return with the dough for a lousy Super Value Meal?

Still feeling the lingering effects of a hangover nearly a week after the Channing–Ava affair, it dawned on me that perhaps I had seen the bottom of far too many cocktail glasses in my time and that perhaps it was time for a change. Then I recalled something the great philosopher Jack Handy once said. . . .

"Sometimes when I reflect back on all the beer I drink I feel ashamed. Then I look into the glass and think about the workers in the brewery and all of their hopes and dreams. If I didn't drink this beer, they might be out of work and their dreams would be shattered. Then I say to myself, 'It is better that I drink this beer and let their dreams come true than to be selfish and worry about my liver.'"

Besides, nobody likes a quitter.

Step 12

Congratulations, You've Completed the Program and Are Now Eligible to Begin a Far Less Glamorous One

"Every now and then you run up on one of those days when everything's in vain . . . a stone bummer from start to finish; and if you know what's good for you, on days like these you sort of hunker down in a safe corner and watch. Maybe think a bit. Lay back on a cheap wooden chair, screened off from the traffic, and shrewdly rip the poptops out of five or eight Budweisers."
—From Fear and Loathing in Las Vegas *by Hunter S. Thompson*

I met Hunter S. Thompson in 1995 in Aspen, Colorado, at a place called the Howling Wolf, a cozy coffee shop-cum-watering hole that at the time was the nexus of the town's political culture. I believe it's a Starbucks now. I was a cub columnist at the local paper and had recently run for mayor in a hotly contested election. Truth be told, most of the heat was generated by the other two, more legitimate, candidates; I was in the mix, it was widely assumed, for comic relief. But as he would later confess, Thompson saw something in me that I certainly didn't know existed at the time, and when he led the charge to defeat a controversial ballot initiative designed to subvert Aspen's long-standing growth-control measures, the Good Doctor enlisted my help to rally the youth vote. We won the ballot vote, and in the course of doing so forged a volatile friendship that I'm now remembering yielded numerous head-busting hangovers, a few knock-down, drag-out brawls out at Owl Farm, his fortified compound in Woody Creek, and—on one particularly harrowing evening—a close encounter with the business end of one of Hunter's pistols.

Hunter was famously fond of his guns, and on a Sunday afternoon in February 2005 he used one of them to take his own life. Why he chose to pull the trigger remains a mystery to me to this day. Despite his oft-repeated belief that confession is good for the soul, he didn't leave behind much in the way of an explanation. He'd had some health problems in the years leading up to his death, and was as volatile a human being as they come. But suicide? *Hunter?* It's hard to believe that all the fear and loathing in the world could ever break the spirit of Gonzo.

As I sit here reflecting upon the day I heard the awful news, it dawns on me that this is the first time I've ever written something about HST without worrying how he'd react to it. The man was fiercely protective of his image and privacy, and anybody fortunate enough to be invited into his circle of friends knew that whatever happened at Owl Farm, stayed at Owl Farm. But I have one memory I think it might be appropriate to recount here.

A few days prior to the aforementioned ballot vote, we hosted a voter registration rally at a nightclub followed by a wild party at the Wolf. Unbeknownst to me—until it was far too late—Hunter had anointed me his designated driver. When I informed him that copious quantities of bourbon had rendered me unable to fulfill that duty, he let loose with an expletive-filled earful, then set out on his own into the night. I arrived home at around six o'clock that morning to find a message Hunter had left on my answering machine half an hour earlier. He'd been busted by the cops for driving under the influence, and was certain his arrest was retribution for our antiestablishment political activities. He wanted me to warn our crew to watch their asses.

"Stay off the streets, for chrissakes," he said in that distinctive mumble of his. "If we're not careful they'll kill us all."

They didn't—kill us, that is—and after a highly publicized trial, Hunter beat the DUI wrap. At a postcourthouse victory celebration, I apologized yet again for my role in the whole ordeal and told Hunter I was glad he'd avoided a jail term that might have derailed our righteous movement.

"Nonsense, bubba," he said. "Nothing can stop this train."

I believed him. Still do. I'm just sad as all hell that our brilliant, mad conductor decided it was time for him to get off.

They say all good things must come to an end, and of late I've been wondering how often that old saw might apply to this book. The part about it being good, that is; there's no doubt it's coming to an end. . . . Having begun this undertaking a good many years ago, it's with a combination of elation and wistfulness that I commit this final chapter to print. I'm just now realizing that I've left some loose ends untied, however, and that the possibility exists that some of you actually give a shit. Here, then, are brief updates on a few of the characters I introduced to you in this tome:

Following our return to the States, Dead Air Dave spent a few lean years bouncing around the Phoenix radio scene until it dawned on him that the desert is really fucking hot. So he split for the cooler pastures of Sacramento, California. The preponderance of those livestock-stocked pastures, combined with the dearth of much anything else in that godforsaken place, apparently drove Dead Air to the brink of madness and, if news reports are to be believed, led him to commit any number of unnatural acts with sheep. He got fired from his job up there, too. Last I heard he'd moved to Europe and was palling around with Count Esconsio in Florenze.

Extremely hot, eardrum-shatteringly loud in the sack, and relentlessly unavailable either to me or the rest of the dudes in my apartment building, my neighbor the Screamer was to sexual conquests what a World Series title is to the Cubs of Chicago—always there and ripe for the picking yet agonizingly unattainable (unless, of course, the boys from Wrigley manage to win the title while this book is in print—in which case, congrats! Yeah, right.). Whenever I fantasized, even momentarily, about bedding the Screamer, and yes, that happened often, I smiled like Boston Red Sox fans the moment it first hit them that they were no longer the sorriest saps in America's pastime.

At this point I should, however, mention that I neglected to fill you in earlier on an interesting bit of information concerning the Screamer. A few weeks after we met, we'd gone out to a local wine bar where, during the course of what would turn out to be a very memorable evening, she filled me in on what she did for a living.

"I'm an adult entertainer," she had revealed, carefully studying me for a reaction as she sipped her cabernet.

"You don't say," I did say, upon which I think my eye twitched or, possibly, popped out of its socket. Unsure of what to do or say next, I smiled nervously and knocked back an entire glass of Inama's Vigneti di Foscarino.*

My guess is that many of this book's likely readership may be intimately familiar with the Screamer's body of work and would no doubt flip were I to reveal her stage name. I'm not gonna do that, though, out of respect for the Screamer's privacy, and because I once got the shit kicked out of me for a similar transgression involving another acquaintance from the adult film industry. Boy, that Rosie Folds packed a mean punch. Rosie and the Screamer aside, I haven't befriended many porn stars, so I can't say with certainty that a majority of them are, in fact, normal. But I can tell you that the Screamer seemed pretty darn well adjusted for a gal who made her living having every one of her orifices breached on camera by magnificently endowed dudes so denoted by names like Buster Hymen and Rod Swollen.

Sure, the Screamer's breasts had been surgically enhanced more times than Joan Rivers's cheekbones, and her Quintuple-Ds got more

---

* Inama comes from Veneto, an old part of the Old World whose wines reflect the area's rich history. Few places in Italy are suited for the production of great white wines, but the fertile volcanic soil in the vineyards around Monteforte d'Alpone yields delightful Soave. Inama's 2004 "Vigneti di Foscarino" Soave Classico is a definitive example of the lively, sweet, and almond-y characteristics of the best Soaves. Vigneti di Foscarino is a very balanced and therefore very drinkable wine. And when I say balanced, I'm talking about a state of harmony between that which is sweet and that which tastes sour—the two main components of any white wine.

exposure than the Hilton sisters. As a result of all the surgery, her nipples were situated up around her shoulders. And because they pointed so prominently skyward, the FAA banned her from wearing tight shirts near airports for fear she'd inadvertently bring down a jetliner or two. All in all, though, the Screamer I knew was a lot like many women: she looked forward to someday getting married and raising a family. She enjoyed traveling, doing yoga, and dancing—sometimes even without pasties and a pole.

Eventually, as is common among those in her line of work, the Screamer was "saved." Not by Evangelical Christians or anything like that, mind you, but saved—literally—from drowning, naked, in a pool filled with Jell-O at a promotional appearance in Lansing, Michigan. So smitten was she with her savior, a brawny pipe fitter from Detroit named Lou, that the Screamer abruptly quit the adult film business and moved to the Midwest. A few months ago I received an e-mail from her saying that she and Lou had relocated to Vegas, where she strips and he deals blackjack. They like to swing, too, the Screamer and Lou.

Glenda the Dirty Ho and Tommy Barnard: theirs was an unlikely union that seemed destined to fail from the get-go, but not even the most pessimistic of prognosticators could have predicted the tragic fate that would befall the West Coast's most notorious hog-riding whore and the lying sack of shit/former best buddy o' mine she fell for. Details are sketchy, but according to a source at the New Orleans police department, Glenda and Tommy were last seen alive sometime around April near the Ninth Ward lean-to they'd illegally holed up in following a quickie wedding performed by a witch doctor in the French Quarter. Neighbors reported that in the months leading up to their end the couple had had several violent encounters, mostly stemming from Glenda's refusal to stop turning tricks. She'd had a storied career as a streetwalker, and in New Orleans she was treated like a celebrity of the sex trade. Her being so in demand fed an insane jealousy that grew and festered inside Tommy. Word has it he was even more pissed at having to pay for Glenda's services even after he put the ring on her finger. Serves the cheap son-of-a-bitch right for going with cubic zirconium.

Glenda couldn't have known what Tommy was planning when he suggested they take the Harley out for a spin one Sunday afternoon, so for the first and, as it turned out, last time ever, she let him drive the bike. The coroner's report concluded that both of them died instantly, which I imagine to be the case almost every time a motor-cycle slams head-on into a tractor-trailer towing a fleet of Lincoln Navigators. When they searched the Ninth Ward lean-to Tommy and Glenda had shared, investigators discovered a sealed envelope he'd left behind. It was addressed to me. Inside was a "Dirty Ho" patch Tommy must have surreptitiously removed from Glenda's jacket, an old photo of Tommy, Sylvia, and me in better days, and a note that read simply, "Thanks for the memories, boss!"

Sylvia up and left without warning and took my heart with her. Okay, that's a bit of an exaggeration, but the truth is I really do miss that woman. She's got a way about her. Don't know what it is, but I know that I can't live without her. She's once, twice, three times a lady: a kindhearted woman who studies evil all the time. We shared the laughter and the tears, and even shared the pain. Hell, Sylvia was the only one who really knew me at all. And while I can't recall if they're green or they're blue, hers are the sweetest eyes I've ever seen. I loved when she breathed out, so I could breathe her in. In fact, I resolved to call her up a thousand times a day, and ask her if she'll marry me in some old-fashioned way. But my silent fears have gripped me long before I reach the phone; long before my tongue has tripped me . . . must I always be alone?

In short, reflecting upon Sylvia is like having a collection of sappy song lyrics stuck in your head. Yet no matter how much I sometimes wish she were still around, in the immortal words of Hall & Oates, she's gone . . . oh, I . . . oh, I . . . I better learn how to face it.

"So this is it, huh?" Bottomfeeder said as, coincidentally, I'd just finished typing those very same words.

I looked up at him and noticed he was drinking one of my beers and wearing my favorite Meat Puppets T-shirt. He smiled at me the way a kid smiles at his mother when he's caught with his hand in the cookie jar and, for the first time in a long while, I smiled back. Behind him near the door sat two suitcases and several cardboard boxes. After five years of living on my sofa rent-free and with full (though never fully granted) access to my food, beer, and cable TV, Bottomfeeder was finally moving out.

"Yeah," I replied, "this is it."

There ensued a long silence during which Bottomfeeder scratched himself and I struggled to reconcile the feeling of relief that came with knowing I was about to be rid of the freeloader with the nagging suspicion that I was going to miss him terribly. It dawned on me just then that the strangest dude I'd ever known—shameless lout and incorrigible rabble-rouser that he was—had pulled some sort of fast one on me over the years and thereby morphed into my best friend. I couldn't say that out loud, not yet at least, so instead I pointed awkwardly in the direction of the beer. Or maybe it was the T-shirt.

"You never really did grasp the concept of *my* stuff, did you?"

He threw his hands up in the air in a mock show of surrender. "Guilty as charged," he confessed. "But I can't help it if I'm a communist, now, can I?"

Of course he couldn't. It wasn't his style. Bottomfeeder didn't just dance to the beat of a different drummer, he played the damn things himself, upside down and with cement drumsticks. Sure, I may have feigned incredulity in this book over his becoming an overnight Hollywood sensation as well as over his many sexual conquests, but truth be told I always knew the guy was destined for greatness. I mean, how many other people do you know who can fart the theme to *Sanford and Son* while gargling single-malt Scotch? Damn straight I'm gonna miss him . . . even with Ava coming out from New York to stay with me for a while.

"You moving in with Kirsten Dunst?" I asked.

"Nah," Bottomfeeder replied as he slung a weathered travel bag over his shoulder. "That didn't work out too well. I probably should have lied when she asked what I thought of *Mona Lisa Smile*. I think she's seeing David Faustino now."

"The little guy from *Married . . . with Children?*"

"Yeah. The prick!"

As it turned out, Bottomfeeder had a new girlfriend named Soo Jin. He met her in the Bay Area on the set of that Seagal movie he did in the wake of the Smirnoff Ice debacle. She's a turbo-kickboxing instructor who served as a technical adviser on the film. While demonstrating some moves for the B-feeder, she accidentally kicked him square in the mug and busted his nose. He claims he fell for her right then and there.

"I'm headed up to Frisco for a few weeks to hang with Soo Jin," he said as he opened the door. "We're going to work on some Democratic fund-raisers, tour Napa, maybe even try and save some endangered species. You know, like the manatees."

"There are no manatees in San Francisco, man," I advised.

"Damn! We're too late," he sighed.

"What about the rest of your things?" I asked him. "Those boxes and suitcases there?"

He inspected them thoughtfully. "I think most of it is yours anyhow. But I'll send for it once I get to Soo Jin's place."

Then there was silence again. I had a sinking feeling in my gut much like the one I imagine Tom Cruise's publicist must have had the moment he got up on Oprah's couch.

"Before you go, I just want to say that—"

"Don't," he cut me off. "I already know. And I feel the same way. Nonsexually, of course. Just promise me something, will ya?"

"What's that?"

"That you won't get gooey and sentimental about all this in your book."

"I won't," I promised. "But you know, man, it really has been quite a ride."

"You're acting like it's all over," he countered. "Truth is, bubba, the adventure is just beginning!" And with that, Bottomfeeder gave me a quick thumbs-up, turned, and walked out the door.

And now the time has come for me to exit as well. Before sitting down at the computer to wrap this up, I flipped through a copy of *Bartlett's Familiar Quotations* looking for a powerful utterance from some great mind to use as an exclamation point to this tome. *Bartlett's* is full of big ideas and inspirational messages, but with all due respect to Gandhi, Ben Franklin, Bob Dylan, and the various other celebrated philosophers in the book, I found what I was looking for from a most unlikely source:

Truth is, bubba, the adventure is just beginning!

THE END

Epilogue

One Tuesday night in August 2004, my mother did something she hadn't done in many, many years: she had a few drinks, and called me the next day to extol the subtle virtues of Frontera Merlot and Amstel Light. When I asked what special occasion had prompted her to lift her self-imposed ban on booze, Mom told me that she and her husband of twenty-three years had been sitting around the house on a warm summer's evening when they suddenly decided to more or less tie one on. It's a touching story under any circumstance: dancing cheek to cheek on the back porch with a long-overdue buzz and her "best friend," she said, was about as much fun as she'd had in years. It's funny how the simplest pleasures can remind us why we call them "spirits" and how much moderate drinking can add to the miracle of every day.

A few nights later, on August 20, six months to the day before Hunter S. Thompson took his own life, my fifty-three-year-old stepfather, John Taylor—a captain in the Philadelphia Fire Department—entered a burning house from which he would not come out alive. He died trying to save one of his men, Rey Rubio, whose gear had gotten tangled up in some wiring in the basement. According to reports, while engulfed in flames and blinding smoke it had become clear to John that they were in dire straits, so he told a rookie firefighter named Bill Studley to grab hold of the fire hose and follow it out to safety. When Bill protested—wanting to stay and help—John sternly "reminded" him that he was the captain and ordered the rookie to get out while there was still time. Then John did something impossibly heroic: he used up every last breath he had in him trying to rescue fire-fighter Rubio. When their bodies were recovered, John was lying behind Rey and it appeared as though he'd been trying to use his shoulder to push his colleague free from the wires. That, my friends, is the ultimate definition of "having your buddy's back."

In the wake of John's death, the outpouring of support for my family was overwhelming. Firefighters from all over the country attended the funeral, along with the mayor, the fire commissioner, and a host of other dignitaries. U.S. Senator John Kerry called my mother to offer condolences; prayer cards from total strangers were delivered in bundles, and a gift arrived from none other than "Rocky" himself, Sylvester Stallone. Ironically, Capt. John Taylor, one of the lowest-key and most private men I've ever known, would have blanched at all the fuss.

I believe this book is something my stepdad would have been very proud of, and I plan to celebrate its completion in a way he would have appreciated: with an ice-cold beer, a glass of Merlot (Frontera, of course), and a heavy dose of Creedence Clearwater Revival, J. T.'s favorite band. I can picture my mother dancing with him on the back porch the night of their impromptu final date, with John Fogerty plaintively serenading the fine couple: "Put a candle in the window, 'cause I feel I've got to move. Though I'm going, going, I'll be coming home soon, 'long as I can see the light."

If you get a minute, I hope you'll raise a glass with us.

Acknowledgments

Without Curtis Robinson's tireless efforts on my behalf, this book would not have happened. Thank you, CR, for being the best editor and friend I've ever had. And if I didn't know she's far too intelligent to ever agree to do so, I'd ask Shelby Sadler to marry me. At the very least, Shelby, please promise you'll work with me 'til death or legal wranglings do us part. And speaking of fine editors, I offer my eternal gratitude to Keith Wallman at Thunder's Mouth for his many invaluable contributions—foremost among them having the good sense to make an offer in the first place. And I shudder to think what sort of hideous experience this would have been without the support and guidance of my beautiful and talented literary agent, Jennifer Unter. . . . And thank you, Alix Strauss, for connecting us. My Hollywood agent, Jeff Aghassi, has stuck by me through thick and thin . . . mostly thin, but certainly not for lack of effort. Hang in there, Jeff—the best is yet to come (I hope). Muchas gracias to Craig Outhier, with whom I have written five unsold screenplays. Here's hoping the sixth one is the charm. Thanks to Caroline Bodkin, Chris Wanjek, and Aurli Bokovza for reading early drafts and offering much-needed encouragement. And I love you, Lisa Hennessy, 'cuz you're one of the most ass-kicking human beings on the planet. Big ups to my boys Z, Moke, Butler, Mysterious Messier, Botox, Art, Joe K, and Craig-O. . . . And, of course, I get hot and bothered just thinking about Steph and Crisi. Terry Sullivan got me started in the booze-writing biz, so blame him for all this. I'm grateful to all the folks I've worked with at Metro over the years, particularly Mark Moore, Steve Morris, Peggy Onstad, Michael Freidson, Kenya Hunt, Nadia Croes, Dorothy Robinson, Per Mikael Jensen, Pat Healy, Sara Hauff, Caroline St. Pierre, and Maggie Samways. Other newspaper and magazine people I've had the good fortune of crossing paths with include Brian Harris, Ed Baker, Greg Trinker, Brent Gardner-Smith, Carolyn Sackariason, Ben Gagnon, David Gadd, Janet O'Grady, Cam Benty, Karen Wittmer, Phil Boas, and the inimitable Dave Danforth. Oh, and thank you, Brian "Pool Boy" Hightower, for facilitating the faux-bear-skin-rug encounter in Aspen. Good times, my friend, good times!

Okay, then, some more fine people worth mentioning . . . Dennis McGlinn, Doug Brinkley, John Oates, Mark Steines, Tommy Lee, Danny Leiner, Dominique Paul, Harrison Starr, Dead Air Dave, JC and Jacqueline, Alli Joseph, Anita Thompson, Beth Lerch, Kimberly Goodman, everyone from *Talk Soup*, Dale de Groff, Sarah Lopez, Tim Beggy, Jessica Beeman, Joe Quigley, Gavin McCrary, Ross Furukawa, all the Philly peeps, particularly Scott Annis, Bob La Brum, Sean McGovern, Ed Dietzel, Billy Nickels, Sean O'Hagan, Jerry Green, Rich Jolly, Marc Dent (aka, the artist formerly known as Captain Nightlife), Andreas Pukis, Ed Ludwig, Ken Knecht, Joe Knecht, Kevin von Arter, Paul McKenna, the Karch brothers, Jimmy Arleth, Steve Miller, Sean Stevens, and Rick Baskin. Special thanks to the Philly firefighters, for everything—Danny Skala, Mike Watson, and the other great guys—for helping my family through a very difficult time a few years back. You too, Mike Dennery. I will never forget it.

And it would be great if you'd buy several copies of this book because I mention you here Meg Noone, Nicole Somers, Jackie Martling, Hammy, Mig and Simone Ayesa, Dave Collard, Jason Auslander, Gerry and Chris Goldstein, the INXS boys, Layne Beachley, Marcos Efron, Wes and LJ, Meg McElwee, Chrissy Doyle, Andre Compeyre, Joanna Brown, Monique Helstrom, Mike Wastvedt, Chris Dodson, Nathan Hatton, Jon Burk, Corey Ackerman, Michelle Gysbert, Jason Forge, Bruce Kerr, Dennis McGee, Jen Tatko, Jeff Pogash, Barry Smith, the Shack crew, Steve Skinner, John Bennett, Amanda Hathaway, Alex Ankeles, Bob Braudis, Kent Smith, Mark Burnett, Ed Calesa, Scott Cru, Sherri Graff, Paul Levine, Wayne Ewing, Bas Pot, Rachel and Mike Bernstein, Willy O' Sullivan and everyone from O'Brien's, Gita Sweeney, Kelly Chambers, Ava Riccio, Cassandra Many, Pete McBride, Leigh Spencer, Meg McElwee, Dan Stadler, Jason and Amber Forge, Deb Pilalas, Monica Martino, Skip Barker, Rob McElhenney, Lucia Pernot, Amy Letourneau, John Carroll, and Shahin Henrikson.

To my beloved Philly sports teams . . . thanks for nuthin', you bums!

To all the girls I loved before.

Thank you, HST, wherever you are.

Thanks to Bono, Edge, Larry, and Adam for making such beautiful music together.

Thank you to everyone I should have mentioned but neglected to. Please don't take it personally. I drink a lot.

Three cheers to my crazy, wonderful, weird family: aunts, uncles, cousins, and all other variations of kin.

And finally, all the love I have to give goes out to John, Lauren, Brian, Sean, and Caitlin. Your strength is my inspiration.

Thanks, Dad. You're my rock.

I love you, Mom. Always.

About the Author

Dan Dunn pens his weekly wine and spirits column, "The Imbiber," for Metro International Newspapers and runs the popular Web site theimbiber.net. He has been a guest on radio and television programs, including *The Henry Rollins Show* and the CBS show *Rockstar*. He is a former staff writer for the TV show *Talk Soup* and freelance joke contributor for *SNL's* "Weekend Update." Dan's work has appeared in *GQ, USA Today,* The *Los Angeles Times, LA Style, Entertainment Weekly, Patterson's The Tasting Panel, Newsday, Hosiery and Underwear Magazine* (really!), and *Aspen Magazine*. He lives in Santa Monica, CA.